# PERCY, BOB & ASSENPOOP

# ELLIOTT BAKER

# PERCY, BOB & ASSENPOOP

© 1999 by Elliott Baker
The Sacred Beverage Press
First Edition, August 1999

"The Portrait of Diana Prochnik" was published in slightly different form in *Unrequited Loves*, G. P. Putnam's Sons, 1973, and Michael Joseph Ltd., 1974.

Part of "The Road Not Taken" first appeared in *Gentlemen's Quarterly*, September, 1991.

**Editors:** Amélie Frank & Matthew Niblock
**Electronic Layout:** Amélie Frank
**Cover Design:** Elliott Baker
**Portrait Illustrations:** Michael Paul
**Baseball Statistician:** Larry Frank
**Matchmaker:** Tom Ianniello, Exile Books and Music

For information on other publications available from The Sacred Beverage Press, please send SASE to:

## THE SACRED BEVERAGE PRESS
### P.O. Box 10312
### Burbank, CA 91510-0312

You can also e-mail us at: Sacredbev@aol.com

**ISBN 1-892687-04-6 $10.00**
**L.C. Card Number 99-072953**

Printed in the United States of America. The publishers would like to thank Sabine Steinmetz and Bill Kirsch of PIP Printing in Burbank, CA (printers for the coming millennium).

Monk by Erica Erdman.

# Percy, Bob & Assenpoop

## Memories of
## Wyndham Lewis
## Robert Frost
## &
## Ezra Pound

The Sacred Beverage Press 1999
Los Angeles, CA

*To Helen*

# Introduction

Having encountered them in my teens, I've been told that I'm possibly the only living person to have known both Wyndham Lewis and Robert Frost. It's an ennobling thought, the kind that gives a delusory sense of significance to one's life. And it's been enhanced by my failure to discover any direct contact between the two men—no correspondence, not a single mention of one by the other, not a shred of evidence that they ever met. That leaves me as a minor link between them, so I defer to the major one.

This, of course, was Ezra Pound, who played so prominent a role in both their lives. His name came up when I was with them, long after he'd seen either, and as I write this his shadow hovers close by. I am in the Kensington borough of London, within a stone's throw of the triangular sitting room from which he once held forth, and only one Underground stop from "Rotting Hill," Pound's term for Notting Hill Gate, later used by Lewis as the title of a book. Also, my block of flats was built on the site where the first V-2 rocket landed and killed one hundred and sixty-two people while Pound was making enemy propaganda broadcasts from Italy.

On a personal level, I once met and exchanged letters with his fellow-poet and loyal friend, William Carlos Williams. The letter I received contained what might be the only rhyming couplet Williams ever wrote and I quote it proudly.

*"You have our academic recorders down pat,*
*But they have us by the balls for all that."*

Williams was "Little Bill" to Pound, "Big Bill" being William Butler Yeats. Pound, In turn, was often called "Assenpoop" by Williams, especially where his political and economic theories were concerned, and I've appropriated this pet name in my title.

My only other connection with Pound has much more remote and tangled roots. These include the film star, Charles Bronson, and Alexander Hamilton and an Arab Prince and a burlesque comic and a male impersonator. And if this assortment doesn't hook your interest, it's doubtful if anything ever will. But let's get the politics out of the way first.

Denunciations of the Jews and President Roosevelt were the core of Ezra Pound's broadcasts. Whether or not his speeches constituted treason was never decided by judge or jury. Whether they were ever heard by anyone but the FBI agents monitoring them has never been established. But the transcripts provided ample material for an indictment.

"There is not one ounce or atom of honesty in either Churchill or Roosevelt."

"The sixty kikes who started this war might be sent to St. Helena as a measure of world prophylaxis."

These are fair samples and his writings were often in the same vein. "The yid is a stimulant and the goyim are cattle," is in *The Pisan Cantos*. But his prejudice had shown some earlier inconsistencies. In *The Guide to Kulchur* he wrote, "It is nonsense for the anglo-saxon to revile the Jew for beating him at his own game." And his American Notes includes "I fail to see why the Jew should commit race suicide merely because Aryans can't think clearly." and "How long the whole Jewish people is to be sacrificial goat for the usurer, I know not."

Nevertheless, his stance during the Second World War was unmistakable. He was anti-Semitic with Fascist sympathies. Perhaps no more so than Henry Ford and Charles Lindbergh, and the father of our thirty-fifth President, but they didn't spout their opinions on Rome Radio. Others who'd used the microphone against the Allied cause, like William Joyce and John Amery, wound up on the gallows. Pound was imprisoned at the end of the war and later interned to await trial. If found guilty, he also faced execution.

I rehash all this because the eyewitnesses to the times are fast diminishing. Dozens of books have since been written about what happened next, about the brouhaha over Pound being given the Bollingen Award for **The Pisan Cantos** and the efforts made by artists and psychiatrists to save his life and the morality debate about whether a great poet is entitled to special treatment. But this is about what happened long before that—before that other great war.

Robert Frost and his family sailed from Boston for England in the late summer of 1912. Pound had arrived there four years earlier with an avowed intent to free English poetry from the shackles of John Milton. He also wanted to meet Yeats and would do both. By the time Frost arrived, he'd already become a thorn in the side of the Bloomsbury group with his campaign to "Make It New." According to T. S. Eliot, Pound was devoting eighty percent of his time to promoting the works of artists and writers he believed in. Many of them, like Eliot and Frost and Joyce, were soon to eclipse him in fame. But as the end of the century nears, Hemingway's prediction at the halfway point that Pound would emerge as its major poet has come true.

Frost didn't mingle in Pound's literary circle, nor did his poems reflect the "new." What the two shared was indignation about artistic achievement being isolated from the mainstream of life in their own country. Pound admired Frost's poetry because it had an authentic voice of its own. He thought it honest and homespun. He also found the poet to be dull, virtuous and pig-headed, but he praised his work in **Poetry Magazine** and vigorously persuaded others to publish it. Though Frost visited him in Kensington at least once, they had little in common and Frost spent most of his time in the country with his family and friend, Edward Thomas.

It was also in 1912 that Pound was first impressed by the drawings of Percy Wyndham Lewis at a Post-Impressionist exhibition. They had met before, the year after Pound arrived in England, but had been wary of each other. It took some time before Lewis discarded his first impression of Pound as a "cowboy songster" and for Pound to realize that Lewis's polemic style and contempt for British philistines equaled his own.

Allowing for intermittent rifts due to clashes of temperament, the two men were to remain united in purpose. Frost's relationship with Pound had no such camaraderie. He was to scribble "Bosh" in the margin of Pound's poem, "portrait d'une Femme," and express ingratitude in a poem of his own.

> *I suspect though in praising me*
> *You were not concerned so much with my desert*
> *As with your power . . .*

Frost returned to America in February, 1915. The following year, Lewis enlisted in the army and the nightmare of trench warfare is reflected in many of his writings and paintings. There was then that prior period of over two years during which Pound could have arranged a meeting between the two. Apparently, he never did. Like Gertrude Stein in Paris, he was careful and omnipotent about who should become acquainted. Frost was eventually to tell William Carlos Williams that he'd avoided him for twenty-five years because of Pound's initial insistence. Similarly, Pound must have decided that, as a trio, he and Lewis and Frost would have produced little in the way of harmony.

What follows may well prove him right. But, at long last, it brings the three of them together.

# WYNDHAM LEWIS
## AND
# THE PORTRAIT OF
# DIANA PROCHNIK

# I

Hemingway said that Wyndham Lewis had the eyes of an unsuccessful rapist. I'm no expert on unsuccessful rapists, but I've met my share and I say Big Ernie was wrong. And none of this nonsense about the cranial pharyngeoma which eventually blinded Lewis giving his eyes a sinister look. The time I'm telling about was years after Hemingway and Lewis met in Paris and there was nothing sinister about those eyes. Lewis blinked a lot, not nervously, but as if to see more clearly. And he kept taking off his round, shell-rimmed glasses and wiping them as if they were to blame. But his eyes were just eyes, except more attentive than most. They didn't shift around. They kept their focus on you as if they wouldn't move on until they'd observed whatever of interest you had to offer. If anything, they were the kind of eyes that discomfit would-be rapists.

So how could Big Ernie, who was sometimes so astute, have been so wrong? And, more to the point, why the eyes? Wyndham Lewis was a man wholly devoted to art. He based his entire life on the accuracy and integrity of his vision. As he said of himself, "My eye is always my compass." So why go after the center of the man? And why an *unsuccessful* rapist?

I'm not going to champion Lewis. I don't know enough about art to praise his paintings and the pet hatreds in his prose are not mine. But his blasting and bombardiering were more than mere noise. Lewis knew his way around a paragraph or canvas and could always spot the genuine article from the fake.

So why did Big Ernie go after his eyes? Remember how they met in Paris. Hemingway was sparring in a gym with Ezra Pound, teaching him the fundamentals, when Lewis came in and watched. When it came to boxing, Big Ernie knew it all. He could vividly describe the technique for sliding a punch and throwing a haymaker and bobbing and weaving and tying your opponent up and crunching his instep and rabbit punching him into another world. But when the fighting starts, words don't count unless you can back them up. And Hemingway couldn't. His brain signaled for the speed and grace of a panther and his muscles delivered those of a foal. Within the squared circle he was like a hoofer in *Swan Lake*.

Take the legends, like that business of socking the editor, Max Eastman. First of all, who couldn't lick Max Eastman? Besides, according to those present, it wasn't much of a punch. More like a lunge with knuckles on the end. The only other guy Hemingway ever flattened was Robert McAlmon who never weighed in at over a hundred pounds soaking wet. Still, Big Ernie could talk a great fight. Morley Callaghan, the Canadian writer, was taken in by this until they went a couple of rounds. That was the day Scott Fitzgerald held the stopwatch and Hemingway lost his temper and started swinging for real and Callagham took him apart.

I don't know how much Wyndham Lewis knew about boxing, but maybe that doesn't matter. Boxing depends on form and movement and impact and these things are an artist's territory. * So there was Ezra Pound swinging like a rusty gate and Hemingway catching everything on his forearms and chattering instructions and Lewis taking it all

* *A letter from Omar Pound to the author (July 8. 1994) includes, "W.L. did a famous painting of boxers at Juan-lea-Pins, & the stances are all correct."*

in. And my guess is that Big Ernie knew he was being seen through, and that's why he went for the eyes. He waited a long time before putting it in writing and it was published after they both were dead. But a one-two combination like "unsuccessful rapist" has been honed by a lot of use in conversation.

What I wanted to tell, though, wasn't Lewis v. Hemingway, but Lewis v. Prochnik, which was something I happened to observe personally. I won't go into the whole history of how Wyndham Lewis got from London to the Hotel Stuyvesant in Buffalo. Briefly, he knew the war was coming and felt there'd be no place for his kind of writing and painting in Britain once the arts there went patriotic. Meanwhile, friends in America kept telling him that he had enough reputation as a painter to succeed there. They were wrong. But he did get commissioned to paint the Chancellor of the University of Buffalo and that's how he wound up at the Stuyvesant, which was a mainly residential hotel on Delaware Avenue. How Diana Prochnik got to the same hotel has never before been told.

## II

We were poor. Not only my family, but the whole neighborhood. The income range was from relief checks to minimum wages. The few schoolteachers among us were the financial elite. So the Prochniks should have moved out years before, when scrap metal turned out to be a good business and Mr. Prochnik and his junkyard struck it rich.

How rich was a bigger guessing game than any quiz show on the radio. There were only three clues: Mrs. Prochnik's full-length mink coat, Mr. Prochnik's Cadillac and the house they lived in. The outside of the house, that is. Nobody ever got invited in. But it obviously was a place that belonged in a better section of the city.

That was one guess why they didn't move. Their house was a white elephant, too elegant for its surroundings, but unable to command the price it warranted because of our crummy neighborhood. Another explanation was that the Prochniks didn't want to move, that they felt comfortable in the house and, their wealth hadn't gone to their heads. After all, except for the mink coat and the Cadillac, there were no signs of ostentation. Mrs. Prochnik only had a colored cleaning woman twice a week when she could have afforded a full-time maid. And their one child, Diana, hadn't been sent away to a fancy finishing school.

I crossed my fingers every time this was said, for I was madly in love with Diana Prochnik. Buffalo, in winter, could feel like Siberia. Without her it would have been even bleaker.

But about being poor. That isn't the same as poverty. The line between them is as thick as between discomfort and pain. Poverty is real pain. Those who have it don't bother putting up a front. They scrabble for coal and lock the door when the landlord comes. But the poor have lots of poses. When the rent's due and they don't have all of it, they threaten to move out unless repairs are made or the place repainted. Or they get into arguments with the local grocers, so they can pretend that's why they're shopping at the super-market.

One of the poses of our poor was the evening gown. Every girl in the neighborhood had one by the time she was sixteen. By then it was a necessity because dances started going formal and dating was their life blood. So, in September of 1939, when *The Sagittae*, which was our Athletic Club, decided to hold a party the vote was unanimous that it be a formal affair.

We had thirty-eight dollars in the treasury, and a committee of three was appointed to find the hotel which would give us the most for our money. The Stuyvesant won. For thirty dollars, it offered a banquet room on the second floor, plus a buffet spread of tuna fish, cole slaw and potato chips.

There were fourteen of us in the club and we probably put as much deliberation into choosing our dates as we later did in picking our wives. Night after night, a group of us would loll around the corner of Ferry Street and Wohlers Avenue, going over the same list of candidates. Our standards varied. Some were partial to those who were rumored to be putting out. Others regarded the invitation as a prelude to going steady. My own choice was simple. I was madly in love with Diana Prochnik. Still, I had reason to worry. Never having said more than a sideways hello to her in school, I wasn't sure she'd know who I was. And there was her wealth. She might think I was after a career in her old man's junkyard.

We all agreed to do our inviting ten days before the party. Five of us met in Pee Wee Potter's kitchen because his folks were out playing Bingo and drew straws for the order in which we'd use the phone. We each had our own technique. Pee Wee Potter's was brief and to the point.

"Is this Phyllis Hunecker? This is Harold Potter. You doing anything a week from Saturday?"

The rest of us spun it out more. We knew that the girls knew we had a reason for calling and wouldn't hang up until they found out what it was. Besides, news of the party could have leaked out, which was all the more reason to make them sweat a little. So there was a lot of gabbing about school and new teachers and what had been done during the summer vacation and Dave Kaplow even went into a long speech about how we should go to the defense of Poland.

My own call was the most awkward. I spent the first minute making sure Diana matched my name to the rest of me.

"Of course I know who you are," she finally said. "You part your hair on the girls' side."

Proof of my love was that she still got the invitation. My hair being parted on the right was a sore spot. Some of *The Sagittae* didn't part theirs at all and some had their partings in the middle. But the rest had theirs on the left and nobody but me and girls had ours on the right. That was how my mother had trained it and years of wet combing and jars of Vaseline hadn't been able to change it.

"John Garfield parts his on the same side as I do," I said.

"Does he?"

"And so does Gene Tunney."

"I didn't mean to hurt your feelings," she said.

"You didn't."

"And I don't judge people by how they part their hair or the color of their skin."

"What do you judge them by?"

"Lots of things."

"For instance?"

"I don't think that's something to discuss over the phone."

"Why not?"

It was hard to hold up my end of the conversation, because the other guys were recombing their hair to change the partings or doubled over and biting their fists so she wouldn't hear them laughing.

"Well, for one thing," said Diana, "I judge people by how honest they are. I place a lot of importance on honesty."

"It's the best policy," I said.

"And I can't stand two-faced people."

"That's sort of the same thing, isn't it? I mean, being two-faced is the opposite of being honest."

"Then how can it be the same?"

I could see why Diana was captain of the high school debating team.

"I guess so. Listen, Diana, I was wondering . . ." And I blurted out the invitation. But she'd sounded so belligerent during all the honesty crap that I'd practically given up hope.

"I'd love to," she said.

"You would?"

I've always been a little unnerved when people accept anything I offer with alacrity. But I remembered to arrange the exact time I'd call for her. We'd be going by cab and I didn't want her to keep me waiting with the meter running.

"I'll be wearing a yellow gown," she said. "Sort of a lemonish yellow."

"That's okay."

"I thought you'd want to know the color."

"Lemonish yellow sounds fine."

"I just thought you'd want to know."

It finally dawned on me that she was hinting about the corsage. But the only yellow flowers I could think of were dandelions and buttercups.

"So, it's a date."

"Yes," she said. "And thank you for calling."

The other guys had recovered from their convulsions by then and were genuinely impressed. I'd asked the prettiest and richest girl in the neighborhood and been accepted.

"Always start at the top," I said.

That Saturday afternoon, a week before the party, all fourteen *Sagittae* marched into Max Mishkin's shop to be measured. It was a milestone we'd been looking forward to. For years we'd passed the shop with the two dummies in the window, one in a tuxedo, the other in tails. At last we were inside and the little man with the big head was bustling around us and getting us to sign the rental agreements. One dollar for twenty-four hours, plus another dollar as a deposit.

Max Mishkin was a whirlwind with a tape measure and straight pins. He cocked his big head at each of us in turn, selected a tux which approximated our size from the rack and soon had the pant and sleeve cuffs the right lengths, the waist tapered perfectly and as much of the back as necessary taken in. Conrad Finkel, who was a skinny six-foot-two and stooped, presented the biggest challenge. The only tux that was long enough hung on him like a tent. But Max, with a mouthful of pins, danced around him and the tent soon fitted like a glove.

The pile of pinned-up tuxedos looked like a lot of tailoring for one man to do in a week. But Max gave us his solemn word they'd all be ready in time, stitched up and pressed like new.

"I don't charge for lipstick smudges," he said. "But cigarette burns come out of the deposit."

The one dollar rental included a dress shirt, cuff-links and studs and a maroon bow tie. The only things left for us to supply were black shoes, black socks and a boutonniere. The shoes were the tough part. Who wore black shoes except married men and undertakers? Some guys had old white summer shoes that could be dyed for thirty-five cents. The rest of us had to borrow a pair. My father wore a 9-C and I was a 10-B, but his patent leather shoes were practically new and when I tried walking in them the pain was bearable.

Pee Wee Potter found a different solution. He had some old white shoes, but didn't want to waste money having them dyed. Instead, he went over them with black shoe polish, adding a new coating every day. By the night of the party, they shined like an eight ball.

Pee Wee and I shared a Van Dyke cab to pick up our dates. Diana lived a block closer to The Stuyvesant than Phyllis Hunecker did, so Phyllis was picked up first. The taxi meter went up a dime from the time Pee Wee went into the house until he brought her out, and another fifteen cents on the way to the Prochniks. Pee Wee looked as worried as I felt. The meter was ticking like a time bomb and we were on a tight budget.

I was hoping that Diana would open the front door, all ready to go. But Mrs. Prochnik let me in and she didn't even call upstairs to tell Diana I was there. She asked me if I wanted a Coca-Cola or anything and Mr. Prochnik asked me if I'd like a real drink and both of them kept sizing me up as a prospective son-in-law while I kept looking at my watch. I looked at my watch so much I didn't make the mental notes my mother had asked me to on how the living room was furnished. There was a white polar bear rug in front of the fireplace with the head still attached and the velvet covered chair I was told to sit down on was purple and everything looked expensive. That was all that sunk in.

"I should mention," said Mrs. Prochnik, "that we'd like Diana to be home no later than midnight." She was a short, heavy woman, proportionately more width than depth. Her shoulders were box-like and her eyes so far apart that they seemed to zero in on me from different directions.

It wasn't until they stood near each other that I realized that she and Mr. Prochnik were identical in size. Had they been of the same sex, they could have swapped clothes. But there all similarity ended. She was as pasty and rouged as he was tanned, as thick haired as he was thinning, as neat in her black dress as he was sloppy in polo shirt and cotton wash pants.

Right after Mrs. Prochnik announced the curfew, we heard the whistle from outside. Pee Wee Potter had the shrillest two-fingered whistle in *The Sagittae*.

"What was that?" Mrs. Prochnik hurried to the window. "It sounded like the police."

"I think it's the taxi driver," I said.

"Taxi drivers whistle?"

"Only when their nuts are hot," said Mr. Prochnik.

"Harry." Her inflection was an apology to me for his coarseness.

"Hey, Diana!" Mr. Prochnik went to the foot of the stairway. "Get the lead out, already!"

"Harry."

"What's she doing up there?"

"Making herself especially pretty."

Mrs. Prochnik beamed proudly at me and Pee Wee whistled again.

"Hey!" Mr. Prochnik yelled upstairs louder. "He's got a cab waiting."

I'd been there almost five minutes and was trying to imagine what the meter read, and trying to think of ways to make it up, like claiming I didn't drink when we went to the cocktail lounge, or talking Phyllis and Diana into going the rest of the way to the Stuyvesant by streetcar.

I got up, as if that would make Diana appear sooner, and suddenly found myself facing Mr. Prochnik. His was a smooth move. He'd planted himself between his wife and me, so she couldn't see his hand go to the breast pocket of my tux.

"No . . . please . . ." I started to take out the dollar he'd put there, but he stopped me with a knowing wink.

"Please, what? What are you doing to him, Harry?"

Mrs. Prochnik waddled over to see for herself just as Diana floated downstairs. She looked even more beautiful than ever before. Her lemonish yellow dress had enough ruffles to be in a Civil War movie, with only thin straps holding it up and a neckline low enough for me to see the beginning of what we used to call The Valley of Desire. But the gardenia corsage I'd sent, because the florist didn't have anything yellow, was already turning brown around the edges.

"Thank you for the lovely flowers," she said.

"You shouldn't have put them in the refrigerator," said Mrs. Prochnik.

Another blast from Pee Wee Potter shook the window panes.

"I guess we might as well be going," I said.

The banquet room on the second floor of The Stuyvesant was smaller than our committee had led us to believe. With the buffet table set up and another table holding Dave Kaplow's phonograph and records, there was only room for half of us to dance at the same time, and then only if the other half stood against the walls.

We took turns, all except Conrad Finkel who said "later" whenever it came around to him. Conrad, who usually stooped at a forty-five degree angle, stayed up against the wall like a West Point cadet. And, in spite of his height and posture, he was the best dancer in the club.

"What's wrong, Conrad?" I waited until I was pressed against the wall next to him before asking.

"Mishkin didn't stitch my jacket," he whispered.

"What?"

"It's still got the pins in. Every time I move, I bleed."

"You can't just stand here all night."

"I know it." He looked ready to cry. "You guys gotta say it's too hot in here and take off your jackets, so I can get out of this."

"But it's freezing in here."

I wasn't exaggerating. The vents at each end of the room were blasting icy air. Diana's smooth bare arms and shoulders had already sprouted goose pimples. Besides, the dress shirts Max Mishkin had supplied weren't to be displayed. The collars and dickeys were passable, but the rest looked like they'd never been ironed.

"Come on, Conrad. Our turn." Edith Seltzer, his date, sidled along the wall toward us.

"Later," he said. "I got a leg cramp."

We were jitterbugging, with Pee Wee Potter ignoring the congestion and kicking up a storm, when the screaming started. Thelma Tanner was the first, staring down in pure anguish at the black smudges on the skirt of her pink chiffon dress. Then Nadine Wirth set up the same noise, pointing to her own dress, and all the others started inspecting theirs. Three more skirts had black streaks.

"It looks like axle grease," somebody said.

It did, a little, and the taxis that brought them were blamed and Dave Kaplow said the cab company would have to pay for the dry cleaning.

"Or it could be black shoe polish," said captain of the debating team, Diana.

And I saw Pee Wee Potter sneaking out the door.

That spoiled the dancing, so most of us adjourned to the cocktail lounge. It was an hour before our time-table called for, because what was left in the club budget only allowed for one drink each. But I was glad. My father's shoes were killing me.

The girls ordered Daiquiris and the fellows Whisky Sours, except for Dave Kaplow who wanted a Singapore Sling. It was while the drinks were being served that I noticed the man at the next table. Not that he was especially noticeable, but his shell-rimmed glasses were not the kind Americans wore. Nor was his tweed suit that looked too heavy for September. 1 found out years later that, having once had a thick crop of hair, he was extra-sensitive about going bald and had all kinds of vibro-massage. But his baldness that night seemed very ordinary. Except, I suppose it made him look more like a bank clerk than an artist.

Diana had the lowest cut dress in the room. She had a beauty mark on her left shoulder that I could have lived without, but otherwise she was as gorgeous as I'd imagined. I was possessive enough to wish there was a little less of her on display and touchy about some of the looks her bare places got from my best friends. So, if the man at the next table had looked at her with a rapist's eyes, successful or otherwise, I would have known it. But, after a first glance, he went back to writing something down in a little notebook. He was drinking brandy.

One sip of their drinks and Dave Kaplow, who went to Bennett High School, and Ralph Bibberman, who went to Hutchinson, started arguing about which school was better.

"Can't we get the conversation on a higher level," said Diana.

"Get her." Ralph Bibberman pulled a stuck-up face.

"She's right." I rose to her defense.

"Who says? What are you, the umpire?"

"Arguing about schools," snorted Diana.

"Okay," said Dave. "What do you want to argue about?"

"Socialized medicine," said Diana. I remembered that was one of the subjects she'd debated the year before. *Resolved that Americans would be healthier under socialized medicine.*

"Jesus!" Dave appealed to the dim chandelier.

"We happened to be stickin' up for our schools," said Ralph. "What's wrong with that?"

"A great deal."

It came from the man at the next table and it shut everybody up. But it wasn't his words or Ronald Coleman accent that did it. He said what he said like he meant it. And that always throws people.

"Pardon the intrusion." The man emptied his brandy glass and went back to writing in his notebook.

"That's perfectly all right," cooed Diana.

"Why is it a big deal?" Ralph had refound his voice.

"The discussion you were having falls into the class of self-categorization." The man closed his little notebook and put it into his pocket. "And that can only be to your detriment."

"Exactly the point I was making," said Diana.

"I don't understand a word," said Dave Kaplow.

"The more you can be made to feel part of a group," explained the man, "the more you can be controlled." I decided that his accent was more Charles Laughton than Ronald Colman. "Your school, your city, your country . . . all these loyalties are exploited by . . ."

We never heard who did the exploiting, because the dumb cigarette girl flounced up to our table with a Speed Graphic and wanted to take our pictures. They cost fifty cents each and that wasn't in our budget. But the girls started shifting chairs and primping, so we couldn't say no.

She took us in couples, one pose each. Then Phyllis Hunecker and Edith Seltzer came in and said they'd looked everywhere and couldn't find Pee Wee and Conrad and would one of us go and get them.

I found them in the men's room, pitching pennies against the wall. The scuffing against the girl's dresses had taken most of the polish off Pee Wee's shoes. Conrad was in a worse mess. He'd tried taking out the straight pins that were scratching him most and his jacket was a tent again. Partners in distress, they'd sworn not to leave the men's room until it was time to go home.

I argued myself blue. I tried to get them to understand how their dates felt. I tried tempting them with the tuna fish buffet, but that didn't work either. It was only when I reminded them that they each had one drink coming and exaggerated the darkness of the cocktail lounge that they weakened.

I led the way back to the lounge and, once inside, they headed for the darkest corner, there to remain with Phyllis and Edith, nursing their one drink each for two hours and refusing to let the cigarette girl take their pictures. Returning to my table, I found the girls on their second Daiquiris and the guys doing mental arithmetic between the bill and what was in their pockets. Our photographs had been developed and put into paper folders and I wished part of the man at the next table wasn't in ours. By then, he was gone.

Thanks to the extra dollar from Mr. Prochnik, I was able to take Diana home by cab. I paid it off and walked her to her front door and kissed her passionately. But she remained as distant as she'd been since I'd come back from the men's room.

"Did I do something wrong?" I'd already asked her that ten times.

"Not at all," she said for the eleventh time. "Thank you for a wonderful evening." I moved in for another passionate kiss, but got straight-armed. "But I was wondering."

"Wondering what?"

"Could you come over Tuesday night?"

Seventh heaven. Midnight bliss in Buffalo. My first passionate kiss had got to her. No necking at the front door for us, where the neighbors could see. Tuesday night her folks would be at the movies or somewhere and we'd have the parlor to ourselves. Or maybe even her bedroom.

"Could you get here about eight-thirty?"

"Eight-thirty on the dot."

"Good," she said. "Mr. Lewis is coming over at nine."

"Mr. Lewis? Who's Mr. Lewis?"

"The man next to us."

"Where?" There was nobody in sight.

"In the cocktail lounge, silly."

"Lewis?" I tried to make the connection.

"He's an artist and while you were off looking for those jerks we started talking. And he wants to paint my portrait. He's coming over to ask my parents about it." She suddenly looked worried. "I think it might help if you're there. I'm sorry I can't ask you to dinner."

# III

She could have invited me to dinner and should have. That was the first thing her mother said when I got there Tuesday night. They were still in the dining room eating, Diana and her mother and father and her cousin Howard who was in his second year of law school and had the smugness of a person who knows his legal rights.

Howard's size and shape, more than his face, linked him to the Prochniks. He had a prematurely lined forehead and the unwholesome pallor of a clerk in a health foods store. He wore a suit with a vest and Mrs. Prochnik kept mentioning this as an inducement to get her husband to put on a tie and sports jacket, or at least a cardigan. But Mr. Prochnik refused. His concession had been a freshly laundered white shirt.

"I don't have to get dolled up," he said, "when somebody's coming to sell me something."

Mrs. Prochnik insisted I have dessert and coffee with them and she was just wedging out my piece of the banana cream pie when the doorbell rang.

"He's early," said Diana.

Nobody moved until it rang again. Then Diana got up and went to the front door.

"We should've been ready in the parlor," said Mrs. Prochnik.

"He can't wait," said Mr. Prochnik. "Business must be good."

Diana brought Lewis to the archway that separated the dining room from the parlor. He still had his hat on and held a huge paper-wrapped parcel. Diana was very correct about the order of introductions. First her mother, who proffered her hand. Lewis had to do a juggling act with the parcel while removing his hat in order to take it. Howard, when introduced, half rose and shook hands, too. But Mr. Prochnik, when it was his turn, just said, "How ya' doin'?" and helped himself to another piece of pie. Diana tried to cover up for this by pointing at me and saying, "And, of course, you remember . . ." I could tell from Lewis's non-rapist eyes that he didn't, but we nodded at each other.

"We're just having a little dessert," said Mrs. Prochnik. "Won't you join us?"

Lewis declined and offered to wait in the parlor. But Mr. Prochnik didn't accept refusals to his wife's hospitality. There was some shuffling to make room for another chair at the table, then he took the parcel out of Lewis's hands and practically sat him down. Mrs. Prochnik gave him what was left of the pie.

"My daughter says you're an artist," said Mr. Prochnik.

"Yes."

"My nephew, Howard there, is in law school."

Lewis turned to Howard as if searching for the link between law and art.

"I looked you up today," volunteered Howard, and Lewis seemed more confused. "In the University library."

"I didn't know my criminal record was on file here," said Lewis. Howard deserved that. Everything he said sounded like a cross-examination.

"You never told us you looked him up." Mr. Prochnik sounded annoyed.

"You never asked me," said Howard. "But since Diana claimed he was famous...

"I'm hardly famous, said Lewis."

"You're too modest," said Howard. His attempted smile came out twisted.

"He's famous?" Mrs. Prochnik leaned back for a fresh survey of Lewis.

"He's in Who's Who," said Howard. He turned to Lewis as if they knew something that the rest of us didn't. "I thought you were only a painter." Did Lewis bristle at the word "only"? "But you've written some books."

"Some books?" chirped Mrs. Prochnik.

"I'm going to read them." Diana made it a solemn vow.

"I'm afraid that will place you amongst the minority," said Lewis.

"What kind of books?" Mr. Prochnik's mouth was dribbling pie while Lewis merely toyed with his portion.

"Essays, stories, a few novels, poetry, philosophy."

"Philosophy?" Mrs. Prochnik again seized on the last syllables.

"Maybe I should'a put on a tie," said Mr. Prochnik.

"Some coffee, Mr. Lewis?" Diana hovered over him with the silver silex. Lewis took it black.

"So you want to paint a picture of my daughter?" said Mr. Prochnik.

"Very much so."

Lewis's answer had a finality to it. There was a long silence as everyone at the table tried to think of another question.

"What's your opinion of Picasso?" said Howard.

"That might be in your library," said Lewis. "I've written about him."

"You like him?" persisted Howard.

"I've said that he is one of the ablest living painters. He's extremely inventive."

"That sounds like you don't think too much of him." Howard sat back and hooked his thumbs in his vest pockets.

"On the contrary."

"Sort of damning with faint praise."

"What the hell was faint about it?" Mr. Prochnik was getting more annoyed.

"I don't know this Picasso," said Mrs. Prochnik.

"He's very modern," said Howard. He seemed ready to elaborate, but Mrs. Prochnik was concentrating on Lewis.

"What do you think of Norman Rockwell?"

"Norman Rockwell? I don't believe . . ."

Before he could finish his disclaimer, she was up and off toward the parlor.

"What about Rembrandt?" Mr. Prochnik had finally thought of a painter's name.

"What about him?"

Mr. Prochnik was saved by his wife coming back with a copy of *The Saturday Evening Post.*

"This is Norman Rockwell."

Lewis wiped his glasses before peering at the magazine she'd thrust at him. The cover showed some old men sitting around a pot bellied stove in a New England general store. Lewis didn't look at it very long.

"He seems to be an able illustrator."

"I hear he gets ten thousand dollars for one of those covers," said Howard.

"Money isn't everything," said Diana.

I expected Mr. Prochnik to correct her, but something else was bothering him.

"You said illustrator. What's the difference between illustrators and what you are?"

"What I am attempts to do more than copy nature," said Lewis.

Mr. Prochnik mulled that over. Then he took the copy of *The Saturday Evening Post* and studied the cover.

"Who else you painted?" His suspicion was showing.

"A number of persons," said Lewis.

"Anybody we know?"

"I've done portraits of Eliot and Joyce."

"Eliot and Joyce who?"

"T. S. Eliot and James Joyce."

"They're writers," said Howard.

"And I've done several of Ezra Pound."

Mr. Prochnik turned to Howard as if for another translation.

"Also a writer," said Howard. He didn't seem anxious to elaborate.

"And Rebecca West." Lewis added it as if to prove that he also painted women.

"You're English." I couldn't tell if Mr. Prochnik was trying to change the subject or if he'd only just placed the Charles Laughton accent.

"Yes," admitted Lewis. "But my father was American."

"Then you're almost one of us."

"Almost." Lewis didn't seem to relish the idea.

"I love the way he speaks." Diana announced it to the world.

"It's just like Claude Rains," said Mrs. Prochnik.

"You ever painted him?" asked Mr. Prochnik.

"No."

"Or the King of England?"

"No."

"Or Neville Chamberlain?"

"No."

"How come?"

"Daddy." Diana's whine was a reprimand.

"What's the matter?" He turned on her. "If he's such a Who's Who painter, how come he's never painted anybody I've heard of?"

"Maybe you've heard of all the wrong people."

"The King of England is the wrong people? The Prime Minister is the wrong people?"

"No," sniggered Howard. "The wrong grammar."

Mr. Prochnik gave him a dirty look. As just an observer, I could have warned Howard that he was flirting with danger, but Diana saved him this time with a giggle. Lewis was looking confused by the whole thing.

"I've brought some of my work to show you." He started to get up for his parcel.

"I'm still drinking my coffee." Mr. Prochnik motioned him to stay put. "How long since you've been in England?"

"Is that pertinent?"

Mr. Prochnik turned to Howard again for a clarification. Howard was racking his head for a synonym, but I beat him to it.

"Relevant," I said.

Mr. Prochnik looked at me as if he couldn't remember what I was doing there.

"So, what do you think?" He faced Lewis again. "Is the war a phony?"

"Of course not."

"Why, of course?" Mr. Prochnik was warming up for an argument.

"No politics tonight, please," said Mrs. Prochnik.

"Mother's right," chimed in Diana.

"Who's talking politics?" Mr. Prochnik's voice got twice as loud. "I'm talking business. Wars affect my business."

"Everything's politics." Howard, trying to be a calming influence, took out a curve-stemmed pipe. "The present conflict is between rival imperialistic powers. And though the aims and objectives of Britain and France may be preferable to those of Germany, I believe that . . ."

"Why don't you shut up?" Mr. Prochnik put all his contempt into the question, then added what sounded like his favorite insult. "College boy."

Howard shrank right in front of our eyes. He'd been summoned for the evening as an expert and told to shut up when he tried to voice an opinion. Disinherited, he toyed with the salt shaker.

"Here's what I say," said Mr. Prochnik. "I say in a couple of months they'll sign a truce and that will be that."

"No," said Lewis. His no had the ring of doom and his face went grave. "I'm afraid the gentler things of life are at an end."

I'd like to think that a pregnant pause followed.

"Then let me tell you something, Mr. Lewis." Mr. Prochnik's lecturing finger stopped in mid-air. "God dammit," he said. "What's your first name?"

"Wyndham," said Lewis.

"Wyndham?" Mr. Prochnik couldn't believe it. "*Wyndham?*"

"It's probably very common in England," said Mrs. Prochnik.

"No," said Lewis. "It's a family name. Actually, my Christian name is Percy."

"*Percy?*"

"Harry," said Mrs. Prochnik.

"Daddy," said Diana. Her "daddy" sounded exactly like her mother's "Harry." I brushed aside a vision of her in middle age.

"If it will make you less uncomfortable," said Lewis, "why not use my surname? Just Lewis, without the mister."

I felt he'd salvaged some dignity by saying this. I'd been sitting there pitying him, the way he was being grilled. I wished I could somehow let him know that he was seeing the Prochniks at their best, that only a doctor, particularly a specialist, would be treated with more respect in our neighborhood than he was getting right then.

"Okay." Mr. Prochnik pushed his coffee cup away as if to clear the table for business. "So you see my little girl at this party . . ."

"Not at the party," corrected Diana. "It was in the cocktail lounge."

"You always hang around cocktail lounges, talking to young girls?"

"It wasn't like that, daddy." Diana was on her feet and looked ready to throw something at him.

"Okay. Okay. So you see her and right away you want to paint her."

"In a manner of speaking," said Lewis. "She's an attractive young lady." I put this down to British understatement. How could anyone only call Diana attractive? But she didn't seem to mind.

"And that's the only reason?"

"No," said Lewis. "I happen to need the commission."

"You work on commission?" Mrs. Prochnik looked disappointed.

"Sylvia." Her name was squeezed through Mr. Prochnik's clenched teeth.

"By commission, I meant fee." Lewis's gentle explanation made her beam.

"How much?" Mr. Prochnik snapped the words. More than good manners had caved in from them.

"That depends," said Lewis, "on the size of the work and the type of portrait. Obviously, a charcoal sketch would be less expensive than an oil painting."

"Obviously," said Mrs. Prochnik. She was still beaming.

"What I can't figure out," said Mr. Prochnik, "is why a painter who's in Who's Who needs dough."

"It's not an unusual situation," said Lewis, "even for artists better known than I."

"Mozart died penniless." Howard broke his long silence.

"Who's talking about Mozart?" Mr. Prochnik waited for an answer and Howard shriveled up again.

"I'm engaged on a portrait now," said Lewis. "But it will be some time before it's completed and I can't very well ask for payment in advance." He was completely matter of fact, not at all embarrassed. "At the moment, I happen to be short of funds."

His frankness threw Mr. Prochnik off stride. He took out a cigar, but didn't offer Lewis or Howard one.

"This portrait you're doing. Of who?"

"The chancellor of your University."

"The chancellor?" Mrs. Prochnik made him sound more important than the King of England or Neville Chamberlain.

"Okay." Mr. Prochnik got up and pointed to the parcel Lewis brought. "Let's see your samples."

We sat around the parlor in the deep sinking furniture, except for Mr. Prochnik who remained standing. And Lewis, of course. After a quick survey of the room's lighting, he moved a straight backed chair in front of the fireplace and used this for an easel.

"Don't trip on the bear's head," cautioned Mrs. Prochnik.

Lewis must have arranged the order of his pictures before coming to the house, for upon opening the parcel he took the top one and set it on the chair for us to see. I expected him to show us some portraits he'd done, but the first picture he put up didn't have a face in it. There were some figures that looked out of Buck Rogers, but most of the painting was taken up by buildings, sort of half skyscraper, half Bavarian castle. There was a horse's rear end in one corner and a moat and some sailboats in the distance. And the colors were muted, with a lot of brown.

I thought starting with this painting was a big mistake. But the way he stood watching all of us staring at it, I wasn't so sure. The painting represented his approach to art and it was as if he'd presented it first to establish where he stood. There could have been a streak of masochism in this, too. The way he waited for our reactions, he looked not only ready to defend his work, but as if he wanted to.

"It's very unusual." Diana finally volunteered the first comment.

Mr. Prochnik was strangely silent. He moved close to the canvas and squinted at it. He touched his little finger to the paint, then backed away as if to get the whole thing in perspective. Mrs. Prochnik, sunk low in the middle of the sofa, addressed her opinion to him.

"Personally, I prefer Norman Rockwell."

"Will you shut up with your Norman Rockwell?"

"Harry."

"Daddy."

Mr. Prochnik waved them both off and moved forward again to inspect the painting.

"This is art?"

It reads like an insult, but it wasn't. It was an honest inquiry.

"It's art," said Wyndham Lewis.

"Not exactly my strong suit." Mr. Prochnik couldn't take his eyes from the painting. "Junk, I know."

"Junk, he knows good," said Mrs. Prochnik and Howard let out a little cackle.

Mr. Prochnik didn't seem to mind. He was grazing his fingertips over the surface of the painting. "What is this stuff?"

"Just oil paint."

"Do you diagram it in first?"

"No. I make some rough sketches."

"Then you just go ahead and paint it?"

"More or less."

"What's it supposed to mean?" Howard resurrected his cross-examining manner.

"What do you mean, what's it supposed to mean?" Mr. Prochnik answered him before Lewis could. "Why does it have to mean anything? It's what it is."

"You have the attitude of a true artist," said Lewis. He said it lightly, but he wasn't kidding.

"Junk, he knows," said Mrs. Prochnik, but this time it didn't get a laugh.

"It's funny.' Mr. Prochnik was talking only to Lewis now. "This time of year, when I go out to my junk yard early in the morning, if the sun is out it looks a little like this part of your picture." He pointed to the most abstract section of the canvas.

"Daddy," cooed Diana. "Your junkyard isn't art."

"Did I say it was?" Her father turned back to Lewis. "But you get this tangle of metal, bashed in cars, rusty girders, everything. And sometimes it's a sort of pattern."

"Could we at least see the rest?" Mrs. Prochnik pointed toward the stack of canvasses and drawings.

"I ain't finished with this one." Mr. Prochnik studied the painting some more with deliberate slowness. "Look," he said to Lewis. "You're dealing with an ignoramus, so fill me in."

"Gladly," said Lewis. "I don't suppose you've heard of Vorticism."

"You suppose right."

"Well, at the risk of oversimplifying . . ."

The following ten minutes or so contained the only lecture on Vorticism I've ever heard, so I've no basis of comparison. Yet, I have a notion that it might have been the best sermon ever given on that art movement. If only there'd been tape recorders in those days and Diana had hidden a microphone in the fireplace. If only I had total recall. As it is, I have only vague impressions to relay.

The most obvious was that none of us had the slightest idea what Lewis was talking about. He used words like boldness and vitality. He spoke of will and revelation and consciousness. These were terms that an evangelist might use on the radio, but no one ever said them in a parlor. And no small part of their fascination, at least for me, was that they were spoken so effortlessly.

I remember, too, his referring to Gaudier-Brzeska. He didn't identify him, assuming I guess that, even in Buffalo, we would have heard of him. We hadn't. Nor did *Blast*, which Lewis mentioned several times, mean anything. One far future day I would come across the first issue of that publication and realize that Lewis had quoted Ezra Pound's definitive lines:

> . . . the twitching of three abdominal nerves
> Is incapable of producing a lasting Nirvana.

I also mention that issue because there was an explanation of Vorticism in it. It boiled down to the domination of the intellect in art and the idea of a painting having a still center. This last rang another bell. I remembered Lewis talking about the center of a whirlpool being still and likening this to Vorticism. Somewhere, he wrote that the Vorticist is not the slave of commotion but its master. "We believe in no perfectibility except our own." I don't know if he said that in the Prochnik's parlor. He might have.

We were all impressed, but to different degrees. For Diana and me, there was the contrast between our teachers who mouthed the curriculum and someone who really knew what he was talking about. Howard's respect was reluctant, almost uneasy. Mrs. Prochnik still seemed more captivated by Lewis's diction than his work or creed. But her husband's attention was the most intense. He kept looking from Lewis to the painting on the chair, frowning to the point of pain. It was as if his face could only be unscrewed by a few clear and simple words. But Lewis made no concession to our lack of knowledge. He could have been talking to the directors of the Metropolitan Museum of Art.

Still, it wasn't just what he said that so impressed us. I'll take the chance of vouching for everybody about that. What was so unusual was that we were listening to a truly dedicated man. Before that night, we'd heard plenty of presumptions to this. After all, we'd already had seven years of Roosevelt's fireside chats. But now we were witnessing the real thing. And one thing any genuine article does is make you aware of all the counterfeits in the world.

Genuine dedication doesn't proselytize. The speaker ceases to be a horn and becomes united with his own words. There is a visible wholeness to the person, an impervious sublimity. Lewis that night was the first man I'd ever seen who knew the substance of his life and was totally content in that knowledge. He had come to sell his talent, but once he began to talk about art, the buyer-seller roles were reversed. What he possessed became the valuable commodity. The wealth in evidence in the room was transitory stuff. Mr. Prochnik had become the subservient party in the negotiation.

Before that bargain was made, Lewis displayed the rest of the sketches and paintings he'd brought. Several were portraits and these were shown last. I then conceded that his order of presentation had been right. The portraits were unlike any we'd ever seen. Had he begun with them, he'd have had little chance to paint Diana. But this way, by the time he showed the portraits, we'd taken our first steps into Vorticism and could tolerate their sweep and hard lines.

"We can hang it over the mantel." Mrs. Prochnik was ready to consummate the deal.

But not her husband. What art was to Wyndham Lewis, bargaining was to Harry Prochnik. His Sistine Chapel was a good buy, and this had its code, too, not the least of which was never to purchase anything sight unseen. A ton of scrap metal was a ton of scrap metal, but no money changed hands until it was weighed. And the same applied to his daughter's portrait. If Rembrandt himself had come into his house, he would have been given the same terms.

These were stated flatly. If Diana wanted to pose for Lewis and Lewis wanted to paint her, it was okay with him. How big the painting and what it was painted with were up to Lewis. Whatever, Mr. Prochnik would pay him one hundred dollars for a satisfactory portrait and he was to be the sole judge of its satisfaction. If he didn't like it, Lewis would get nothing.

"I seem to have no choice," said Lewis, "but faith in my own ability."

"And another thing." Mr. Prochnik specified the extra clause to Diana. "Whenever he paints you, I want your mother there."

I maintain that there was no undue suspicion in this, that in those days any father of a beautiful sixteen year old girl would have insisted on the same thing no matter who the artist was, that Harry Prochnik did not see in Wyndham Lewis's eyes what Ernest Hemingway claimed was there.

# IV

Lewis had rented a room with a skylight on North Street to use as a studio and twice a week Diana, accompanied by her mother, went there after school. I got regular progress reports by stopping at her table in the cafeteria. Not that she had much to report. Lewis wouldn't let her or her mother see what he was putting on the canvas. Mrs. Prochnik had tried to sneak a look once and been told off. According to Diana. Lewis went absolutely purple, so neither of them tried again. But the suspense was killing.

Then, after about three weeks, Diana stopped me in the corridor between classes to let me know that the portrait was finished and Lewis was bringing it over that night. I kept saying that I was dying to see it and reminded her that I'd been in on the beginning of it, but she didn't invite me to the unveiling.

I was so pissed off about it I couldn't concentrate on my homework that night or even the radio. All I could think about was what was going on in the Prochnik parlor. Diana's not inviting me had become an insult. I resolved not to have anything more to do with her, never to speak to her again. Men had given up their true loves for less. I decided to go to bed early and was half undressed when the front doorbell rang. It was almost ten o'clock. Only telegrams arrived at this hour. I wondered which relative had died.

"You got the girls chasing you now." My father came into my room to tell me I was wanted. "She wouldn't come in," he said. "She's waiting outside."

"Who?"

"The Prochnik girl. She's a real looker."

I went out in the old clothes I'd just taken off, without Brilliantine on my hair, without Sen-Sen for my breath, because I figured it had finally dawned on her that she'd insulted me and had only come to apologize. I was just going to be offhand and laconic, so how I looked or smelled to her no longer mattered. But my anticipated conversations have never materialized. How can you be offhand and laconic to a girl who's practically hysterical? Diana kept wringing her hands and letting out little bursts of words that didn't connect.

"So humiliating . . . wanted to die . . . never in my whole life."

I suggested a hot chocolate at Stern's Delicatessen because it had booths at the back that nobody ever used.

"No," she said. "I'd rather walk."

She took my arm, not in affection as much as to steady her, and we went towards Humbolt Park. On the way, she told me what had happened.

Lewis had arrived with the portrait carefully wrapped. He'd seemed very confident, more light-hearted than she'd ever seen him. He'd moved the same chair in front of the fireplace to use as an easel.

"Before we get to that," said Mr. Prochnik, "there's something I want to ask you."

Instead of asking it, he went into the kitchen and out the back door to the attached garage where he parked his Cadillac. Diana couldn't wait to see her portrait and neither could her mother. So, after waiting about a minute, Mrs. Prochnik told Lewis to go ahead. And he was just unwrapping the paper when Mr. Prochnik came back in with an armful of canvases.

"Here. Look at these."

He took the still unexposed portrait of Diana off the chair and replaced it with one of the canvases he'd brought in. Each of them was displayed in turn. Every time Mr. Prochnik put up a new one, he stepped back and looked at it admiringly before turning to Lewis to see his reaction. But Lewis never showed one.

As for what was on the canvases, I have only Diana's word.

"Awful."

We were walking in the park by then. It was empty and dark and I steered her towards the most concealed bench as she went on. The canvases were supposed to show various views of Mr. Prochnik's junkyard—twisted metal, crushed cars, old gates and railings, even sections of street car tracks that had been dug up.

"They were mostly black and rust," she said.

"I guess most junk is," I said.

Studies in black and rust. A Vorticist view of junk. Without his family knowing, Mr. Prochnik had bought an easel and tubes of paint and countless clean white canvases, framed and drawn tight. And those mornings when the sunlight slanted across his junk yard in just the right way, he'd painted that which he knew best and relished most.

"And they were pretty awful, huh?" I had my left arm along the back of the bench and was gradually drifting it toward her shoulders.

"Not that he asked me my opinion," said Diana.

Nor his wife's. The only judgement Mr. Prochnik wanted was from Wyndham Lewis. And, after the last and largest of the paintings had been placed on the chair, he waded into the other man's silence.

"Well? So what do you think?"

"What exactly do you want to know?" said Lewis.

"I want to know what you think." Mr. Prochnik tapped the painting on the chair. "Of this one, especially."

"And what did Lewis say?" As I prompted her, my dangling left hand grazed the mound of her left breast.

"He said . . ." Diana pursed her lips in concentration, determined to quote him exactly. "I assume these are of your place of business."

"You can tell that?" Mr. Prochnik took it as a compliment. "But what about art?"

"Art?"

"How do you rate them as art?"

Lewis had been so mild and polite up to then, that they weren't prepared for what happened. The way his face went purple again was a warning to Diana, at least in after-thought. He'd looked like he was going to have a stroke right there and then.

"What do you think art is, a pastime?"

The question wasn't asked, it was thundered. This made Lewis's face flush even more and it was as if its color was taken from Mr. Prochnik. The purpler Lewis got, the paler her father did.

"Wow!" I said. "Imagine." I'd cupped her breast by then and she hadn't even squirmed. The six buttons down the front of her green sweater loomed like the combination to Fort Knox. My free hand crawled towards the top one.

"What do you think art is?" repeated Diana. "A weekend amusement for hungry vanities? A nursery where the idle can dabble?"

Lewis picked up the most ambitious of Mr. Prochnik's canvases, holding it at arm's length as he looked at it, as if it were contaminated.

"You know nothing of pigment, nothing of composition, nothing of form or texture." Diana interjected that Lewis's voice was positively trembling with emotion. "You make a few vulgar scrawls that any child could make and you want to be praised for it. Men devote their entire lives to art. Men starve and suffer and die for art. And no one has the right to cheapen and denigrate what others die for."

"He said all that?"

"Every word," said Diana.

"Some speech." The top button was undone.

By the time Lewis finished, he was breathing heavily. And during his tirade, the color started leaving his face and returning to Mr. Prochnik's. When he grabbed his most ambitious painting out of Lewis's hands, his blood pressure had hit a new high. But, for the first time in his life, he didn't yell back. He just pointed to the wrapped portrait Lewis had brought.

"Okay," he said. "Let's see yours."

"And how was it?" Button number two bit the dust.

"It took a little getting used to," said Diana. "Of course, everybody was upset anyway so it was hard to be objective and it wasn't supposed to be a completely true to life portrait. It didn't have every eyelash."

"Not every eyelash, huh?" Two of my fingers started down The Valley of Desire.

"But what it did capture," she said, "was my soul."

Up to then, beautiful as I thought she was, I'd never given any thought to Diana's soul. But Lewis, with his artist's vision, had not only seen it, he'd captured it.

My hand, wrist and arm had reached an awkward angle. While I was trying to rearrange them for my next move, Diana started going on about her eyes in the portrait not being as blue as they really were and her hair being too dark.

"Still, he got your soul right."

"It's amazing," she said. "It's like he could see right through me."

That was something I'd been trying to do for a long time. Not through her, just her clothes.

"He could, huh?"

"It's hard to put into words," she said. "I look very thoughtful in the portrait."

"You do?" I was mustering up courage for my big move.

"It's as if I'm going to cry."

"But that isn't what you're like."

"You mean you don't think I'm thoughtful?"

"I mean the crying. You're always cheerful."

"That's just a front I put on."

"I know you're very thoughtful."

"My mother always says I brood too much."

"What did she think of the painting?"

Diana didn't know. Mrs. Prochnik never had a chance to say. Nor did Diana, at least not to Lewis. After the painting was unwrapped, she felt she should study it for awhile before saying how she felt about it. But Mr. Prochnik didn't need any time to make up his mind.

"It's crap," he said.

"Daddy."

"Harry."

"Crap! I wouldn't give two cents for it. I wouldn't have it in my house if he paid me!"

Nothing more had been said. Diana breathed a sigh of relief about that. Wyndham Lewis was a big man. Harry Prochnik, short and dumpy, was muscular. Diana was sure that if one more word had been spoken, there would have been a fight, right on their white bearskin rug. But total silence had descended on the Prochnik parlor. The paper didn't even seem to rustle as Lewis wrapped it around the portrait, and he didn't slam the door when he walked out.

I felt the anti-climax. Somehow it dimmed my own passion. The night air was suddenly cold, The Valley of Desire moist. So when my hand moved on, it was more to resurrect my desire than propelled by it.

"I can never go back to that house," she said.

"I love you," I said, and slid my hand inside her brassiere.

She looked at me before she leapt. She managed three expressions in less than a second, the first thoughtful, the second as if she was about to cry and the third pure horror. Then she leapt. Maybe it wasn't an Olympic broad jump record, but she did it from a sitting start.

"You." She breathed at me exactly as she'd been imitating Wyndham Lewis's breathing. "What do you think you're doing?"

"I was trying to capture your soul." I could feel my disarming smile falling apart. "But I guess I missed."

"I suppose you think that's smart."

"I love you," I said. I tried to make it sound everlasting even though my wrist felt dislocated by her leap.

"You're like all the rest," she said. "I thought maybe you were different. But you've got a dirty mind like all the others." She turned and stamped away toward the lights of the street.

"Diana!" Her jump had popped a button off her sweater. I picked it up and trotted after her.

"The only thing different about you . . ." She stopped and turned and measured me in her sights. ". . . is the way you part your hair."

Wyndham Lewis died in 1957, and if I owned one of his paintings now I could retire. Ernest Hemingway shot himself in 1961. Harry Prochnik succumbed to a heart attack around the time of Hiroshima. The last I ever heard of Diana, she was married to an osteopath and living in Miami and her mother was with her. So only her portrait remains unaccounted for. I went to a retrospective exhibit of Lewis and the Vorticists at the Tate Gallery and it wasn't there. I've found no reproduction of it in any of the coffee table books of modern art.

Most likely, short of cash and canvas, Lewis painted over it and it lies dormant under one of his abstract interpretations of our world. Maybe, someday, it will be detected by X-ray, or the outer layer will peel off and Diana's face will emerge. Maybe it will eventually find a place on a gallery wall and the art-loving public will shuffle by and wonder who she was, and the art experts will bring in a verdict on the one permanent embodiment of my dreams; *Portrait of a Girl, circa 1939.*

(From a letter by Wyndham Lewis to Charles D. Abbott.)

## HOTEL STUYVESANT

## BUFFALO

### A House of Homes

(Sunday)

Oct. 15, 1939

(The cocktail parties you foresaw me frequenting have not materialized.) The likelihood therefore of the portrait of Dr Capen leading to other portraits appears to be slender. That is rather disappointing as I had hoped to make Buffalo my headquarters for a further month or two. Still, we shall see. If by next Thursday nothing happens I shall know that without your magic wand the Buffalo is an animal inaccessible to artistic stimulus.

.

# ROBERT FROST
## AND
# "THE ROAD NOT TAKEN"

# I

Miss Delahunt used most of the blackboard for the poem, writing it large so the whole class could see it. She made us recite it in unison, over and over, I don't know how many times. But even now, I can still do it word-perfect, all four stanzas of it, from "Two roads diverged in a yellow wood" to "And that has made all the difference." Miss Delahunt had added his name at the end of it and that was the first time I heard of Robert Frost.

Five years later, in the early spring of 1943, he came to Bloomington, Indiana to conduct a three week seminar at the state university there. I was writing poetry, too, by then. My favorite device was to discover an obscure word, preferably of four or more syllables, and rhyme it with a simple one: teratologist with mist, things like that. I knew I'd be going into the army when the semester ended and that flavored my verse, soldiers nailed on sprays of flame and blood bubbling from young murdered mouths. I applied for the seminar and submitted the required three samples, but I didn't really expect to be accepted. I was on campus to play baseball because my high school coach in Buffalo knew the Hoosier's coach, "Pooch" Harrel, and I'd been shoved into the School of Business because I didn't have the entrance requirements for the finer things in life like Liberal Arts. So when the postcard came saying I'd been admitted to the seminar I felt that someone in the English Department had been very impressed by my three poems.

The seminar was to meet on Tuesdays and Thursdays from two to three. Baseball practice had begun by then and when I told the coach why I'd be a little late on those days he gave me a funny look. The one hour sessions were held in a second floor room in Ballantyne Hall that needed repainting. We sat around a large rectangular table with Frost at the head. The photographs of him in the copy of *North of Boston* that I'd found in the library had been taken in England in 1913. The handsome profile and studied pose didn't go with his poems. But the first day of the seminar was only a few short of his sixty-ninth birthday and by then he'd perfected that craggy, rustic image that served him well with the Pulitzer Committee and which he'd leave with the world.

He mumbled a lot, looking less at us with those hounddog eyes than out the window which he always wanted left open. "Keep your hand busy," he said that first day, and "You can't write poetry all the time." In later sessions he became more profound. "Poetry provides the one permissible way of saying one thing and meaning another." He stayed silent until we'd all carefully written that down. "Grievances are a form of impatience. Griefs are a form of patience." That was another one for our notebooks. "Poetry is tropism in the sense that biologists use the word." That one stopped us cold. Tropism and schism were soon to join teratologist and mist in my collected works.

I expected him to read some of his own poems to us. I wanted to hear "Birches" or "Fire and Ice" and, most of all, "The Road Not Taken" in that gravelly drone of his. But he kept rambling on about metaphors and the only poem he recited that first week was Edwin Markham's "Outwitted."

> He drew a circle that shut me out—
> Heretic, rebel, a thing to flout.
> But Love and I had the wit to win:
> We drew a circle that took him in.

I didn't know then of his passion for baseball. It surfaces several times in Lawrance Thompson's biography of him. There was a time when he was teaching at Amherst or Ann Arbor when a big league pitcher lived next door and Frost used to catch him during the off-season, just easy stuff in the driveway between their houses. If Frost ever had "aspirations" I hope he wanted to be a catcher because that would give a little extra to what happened between us. If he'd wanted to be a catcher he'd have had to admire Mickey Cochrane as much as I did.

The rains ended early that spring and baseball practice had already moved outside from the fieldhouse. It was my junior year and I was to pitch first-string unless some buck-toothed, coil-armed farm kid showed up out of nowhere. "Pooch" Harrel didn't go much on bunting and base sliding techniques so practices soon developed into three inning games. It was during one of these that I noticed Frost among the smattering of those watching from the bleacher benches. I got the third out on strikes and he was watching me as I came off the mound. It was hard to tell with those craggy, hound dog eyes, but I thought he gave me a congratulatory wink.

After that I felt he was a little more aware of me in the seminar than he was of the others. We'd reached the point where he was letting us read some of our own efforts. He never criticized them. An "mmmm" was as close as anything got to praise and wasn't heard often. Each Tuesday and Thursday I showed up with what I considered my best poems and eventually he got around to me. I was sitting close enough for him to see the full-page, single-spaced one I'd decided on.

"Something nice and short," he said. So he only got second-string.

> *Born with or without a silver spoon,*
> *(It may be stainless steel now)*
> *Your father appeared as a mawkish baboon,*
> *Your mother a maundering cow.*

A few of the students laughed but Frost just stared at me from under his bushy eyebrows. I still thought my poem was better than Edwin Markham's "Outwitted" and plugged on.

> *Gummy, pink spermatophore,*
> *Howl and stink and wet the floor.*
> *If a girl you'll be a whore.*
> *If a boy you'll go to war.*

My memory is of a room filled with discomfiture. None of the other students had produced anything remotely shocking and, in those days, words like whore were confined to beered-up Saturday nights. And I wanted to shock. Wasn't that what the unacknowledged legislators of the world were supposed to do? I didn't expect to get an "mmmm" from Frost. But I wasn't prepared for a pitying look either.

"You'll feel better when you're older," he said.

He was right, of course, but it hurt. It hurt sporadically for years. It takes a long time to reach that point he'd long passed, when you don't cry over not getting an extra moon you wanted. But Robert Frost didn't know how to make words hurt the way Mickey Cochrane did.

## II

Any short list of great catchers includes Cochrane along with Bill Dickey and Yogi Berra of the Yankees and Harry Danning of the New York Giants. Mickey Cochrane was extra special because he was a player-manager and led the Detroit Tigers to the American League pennant the first two years he managed them. None of the sports writers gave them a chance in the World Series against the Cardinals the first time. The 1934 Gashouse Gang of St. Louis looked unbeatable. The Dean brothers, Dizzy and Paul, were going to mow the Tigers down. If it hadn't been for Cochrane, they might have. He was all over the place, playing like a man possessed and Detroit took the series the full distance.

During my teen-aged years, before I'd ever heard of Robert Frost, I hero-worshipped Mickey Cochrane. I'd lost track of him by that spring of 1943. He'd retired as an active player in 1937 after being beaned by Bump Hadley and left the Tigers a year later. I didn't know he was in the Navy until "Pooch" Harrel broke the news about the Great Lakes Naval Training team coming down from Chicago for an exhibition game with us and mentioned that the great Mickey Cochrane was managing them.

The Great Lakes team was strictly a safe depository for major leaguers, one of those special creations the armed services set up to make sure that no top athlete or movie star got killed in action during the war. I don't believe any did, though Barney Ross came close at Guadalcanal and James Stewart flew a number of missions over Europe. Mickey Cochrane was too old to be drafted. But they'd made him something like a Lieutenant Commander to manage the Great Lakes team.

The game was the following Wednesday and there were dreams of glory in the little sleep I got the night before, of big leaguers swinging like barn doors at my breaking stuff and the winds of fate which determined scratch hits and Texas Leaguers blowing our way. The world had seen bigger upsets than a college team beating a fancy collection of pros.

Cochrane was on the field right from the start of the pre-game practice. He looked pretty paunchy, his hair graying but thick, and he still had that special leathery tan that ball players have. While everybody else watched Benny McCoy at second base because he'd been the highest paid bonus player in history, I kept my eyes on Cochrane hitting fungo flys to his outfielders. He looked like he could do it with his eyes shut but the exertion reddened his face.

I came close to walking across and introducing myself and asking him for his autograph. But there was a grimness about him that stopped me. One fielder came up short on a fly ball and Cochrane barked at him to wake up or he'd find himself on a mine-sweeper. He made his players hustle even if he had to pull rank to do it. He couldn't have looked much grimmer in that seventh and final game against the Cardinals. This was a ball game and ball games were meant to be won.

I finished my warm-up and "Pooch" Harrel and Cochrane went over their lineups with the home plate umpire and the bleachers had never been so full. This was the time I always got the flutters. Kicking some dirt around on the mound usually shook them off but not that day. I took my time with the resin bag and avoided looking toward the Great Lakes players. The smallest guy on their team looked bigger than any of us. Their brand new uniforms helped. Ours were faded and a little shrunk from launderings. So I looked at the crowd instead while I rubbed up the ball. It was mostly of students and solidly on our side, a lot of the shouted encouragement aimed at me. Then I saw Frost and that bothered me. If I was going to get creamed, which I undoubtedly was, I could take a couple thousand students seeing it. But I didn't want him to see it.

He was sitting right down front behind third base and Mickey Cochrane was trotting to the third base coach's box and for the first time in my life I wished I'd been born left-handed. Southpaw pitchers have one big advantage. In a no windup situation they're facing their own bench. But with men on base, and there'd be plenty of those, I'd be looking toward the Great Lakes bench and Mickey Cochrane and Robert Frost.

Bench joykeying had never affected me much. In high school and college games it had been mostly "He's got nothin' on it" or He's thrown' garbage." Sometimes the garbage was changed to crap but that was about as rough as it got. I expected worse from the Great Lakes bench but their players were strangely subdued and Cochrane in the third base box seemed totally unaware of me. He just chirped encouragement to Benny McCoy who was stepping up as his lead-off man. "Here we go! Everybody hits!" He kept up the nice, clean, All-American chatter and I got ready to throw to a guy who'd been paid forty-five thousand dollars just for signing with Philadelphia. Then my great boyhood idol started on me.

He had the kind of rasping, high-pitched voice that a lot of heavy-set athletes have and when he made a megaphone of his hands it didn't lower much.

"What we got us out there? Hey, beanpole, get your ass back to your dancing class!"

Ass to rhyme with class. It wasn't much worse than Edwin Markham, nothing to rattle me so far except his shrill voice.

"Look at what we got us . . . a solid shit beanpole!"

I should have acknowledged it with a stony glance or even stuck out my tongue. Then he might have stayed on me. But I just leaned forward for my catcher's sign so he started on my mother.

"How's your old lady, beanpole? I hear she's a great lay! I hear she'd fucked every bum in Indiana!"

My first pitch went into the screen behind the plate.

"You got any sisters, kid? Mama teachin' them the tricks of the trade? They out whorin' aroun', too?"

I threw one more pitch that had to be dug out of the dirt before starting toward him. Kermie Wahl, our third baseman, made a half-hearted move forward to intercept me but Cochrane just stood waiting, his hands on his hips and slowly chomping gum. I never intended taking a swing at him. I knew he'd do to me with one punch what he'd done to the Cubs in the 1935 World Series. So I stopped well out of range and he stood there waiting with those steel blue eyes that had unflinchingly faced the best fast balls and sliders ever thrown.

"My mother's never been to Indiana," I said.

"G'wan," was all he said.

"Play ball," snapped the home plate umpire and I went back to the mound.

Since it was only an exhibition game there's no record of it in the Navy archives. I phoned the chief Naval historian in Washington to check that out. So, maybe I could get away with lying about the final score. But for the sake of posterity it was Great Lakes 15, Indiana 2. I was only charged with four of their fifteen runs. After I walked the first four batters on sixteen consecutive pitches, "Pooch" Harrel took me out. Just about the lousiest minute of life is while you're waiting for your relief pitcher to walk in from the bullpen. Dale Shoemaker who took over hadn't had much time to warm up but he had the comfort of knowing he couldn't do worse than I did. I got a few handclaps and some boos as I went to our bench, but Cochrane's high voice cut through them. He was already starting on Dale Shoemaker's mother.

The next day saw the last of our poetry seminars. At the end of it one of the students finally asked Frost if he would recite a poem of his own. He shook his head at first, then changed his mind.

"I'll give you a part of one," he said. He took his time starting as if reciting what led up to it to himself.

> *Eyes seeking the response of eyes*
> *Bring out the stars, bring out the flowers,*
> *Thus concentrating earth and skies*
> *So none need be afraid of size.*
> *All revelation has been ours.*

He said goodbye to us individually, shaking each student's hand, and each muttered something about enjoying the sessions. I made a point of being the last. His hand was surprisingly soft for someone who'd written so much about fields and farms and mending a wall. I wanted to say something more personal to him than any of the others had.

"I had a high school teacher," I said "who wrote all of "The Road Not Taken" on the blackboard one day . . ."

"Mmmm." He didn't wait for me to finish, ignoring what I'd said the way people who've already received a lot of praise do. He glanced past me to make sure all the other students were gone. "If that bastard said those things about my mother," he said, "I'd have gone after him with a bat."

"I didn't have a bat," I said.

"In a baseball game there's usually one around."

### III

I was often aware of Frost in the fifteen years that followed, of new volumes of poems published and additional honors received. He was good interview material for the Sunday morning television shows which were the networks' concessions to literacy and I saw him on a few. During one of them he said that poetry is tropism in the sense that biologists use the word.

In 1958 I also wanted to exploit him on television. I was doing a documentary film for CBS about the conformity amongst college students which seemed a residue of the McCarthy era. My notion was to epilogue the program with his reading "The Road Not Taken," its last three lines summing up my theme.

> *Two roads diverged in a wood, and I—*
> *I took the one less travelled by,*
> *And that has made all the difference.*

It took some doing but I managed to get his phone number in Cambridge, Massachusetts. He answered the phone himself and I explained why I was calling and said we'd sort of known each other fifteen years before.

"My memory isn't what it was." He sounded about to hang up.

"Mickey Cochrane." I said the name in desperation.

"Mmmm. Played for Detroit."

"That's right." I said. "And you told me I should have hit him with a bat. And if you'd lied a little and said something encouraging about a poem of mine, I'd be teaching English Literature at Vassar or Bennington instead of slaving in the salt mines of television."

"Did I do that to you?"

As it turned out, he was to soon be doing a reading at nearby Rutgers University. I said we could film him reciting "The Road Not Taken" immediately afterward. The clincher was the five hundred dollars I'd been authorized to offer him. It was probably twice what he was getting from Rutgers.

Everything was arranged to make it as easy for him as possible. As soon as he finished his encores in the Rutgers' chapel he was ushered across to the classroom we'd set up for the filming. He was obviously tired but unhesitatingly signed copies of his books for those members of the crew who'd bought them. He didn't pretend to remember me but inscribed my copy as if he did. Then I positioned him in front of the black backdrop we'd hung and the cameraman took his light reading and moved the key lamp a few inches and we were ready to roll.

"Just what do you want me to do?" Frost looked troubled and turned to me.

"Only 'The Road Not Taken.'"

"I can't do it cold," he said. "I'd better work up to it from one of the others."

It was an unexpected bonus, but of no use in the documentary.

"Or you could talk about the poem itself," I said. "About when and where you wrote it and what inspired it."

He liked my suggestion and began. Luckily, both the camera and sound men had already switched on.

"In 1914 we were in this farmhouse in Gloucestershire," said Frost. He decided to add "in England" as if aware of American audiences' limitations on foreign geography. "It was summer, but we needed a log fire some nights. And we were sitting around this big, open fireplace, my friend Edward Thomas and his wife Helen and Elinor and me, and it was right after we'd heard that war'd been declared. Edward thought he should join up right away and then he thought maybe he'd better wait a little. He was always like that when he had a decision to make, weighing this and that, looking one way and another for a long time before choosing what he'd do. So the poem came less from me than from him."

He recited it then and I can't believe he ever did it better. His biographer, Lawrance Thompson, was there and he said as much to Frost when it was over. Then the three of us went to the apartment of one of the university deans who was an old friend of Frost. He had prepared some food but Frost didn't want any. He was still keyed up from both the chapel reading and the filming and full of talk. Lawrance Thompson jotted down some of the things he said.

Frost got around to Ezra Pound, but mostly to tell about his part in getting him out of his internment in St Elizabeth's hospital. It had been more than six months since Pound's release and he was still relishing how he'd done it.

"The New York Times said it took me two years. But they exaggerated a little, the way newspapers do. Two minutes was more like it. I just walked into (Attorney General) Roger's office and asked him what his mood was in regard to Pound. And he said. 'Our mood is your mood: Mr. Frost.' And I said, 'Then let's get him out right away.'"

He'd accomplished what Archibald MacLeish and Ernest Hemingway and T. S. Eliot, combined, hadn't been able to. He couldn't help crowing over that. Then he felt like a walk and asked me to go with him.

It was a clear night. November had swabbed most of the trees and the leaves crackled under our feet. I wanted to hear more about Edward Thomas who'd taken the road of patriotism and been killed in action. But Frost was still going on about Pound.

"He sneaked up behind me in that pub'," he said. "He never could have thrown me otherwise." He couldn't recall the exact circumstances. But it had happened in London when Pound was first succeeding in getting him published.

I mentioned a line of Pound's I'd come across, to the effect that if a man wrote six good lines of poetry he was immortal. Frost seemed to be considering it as we walked on.

"Six is about right," he finally said. We'd reached a corner and had to wait for some cars to pass. "And how many you done so far?"

"Only four," I said.

"All right. Let's hear them."

He turned to me and waited. He was serious. I had no choice but to recite loud and clear above the traffic noise.

> *Born with or without a silver spoon,*
> *(It may be stainless steel now)*
> *Your father appeared as a mawkish baboon,*
> *Your mother a maundering cow.*

I didn't want a lousy Mmmm. All I was hoping for was a flicker of memory in his face, The closest I got to it was the same pitying look the lines had earned me fifteen years before.

"I guess I deserved that," he said.

## IV

I never saw him again after that night, but I recently dug out the note I received from him a week or so later. It was sent from the Homer Noble Farm in Ripton, Vermont and dated November 29, 1958.

> "That was a fine evening we had together, ideas, reminiscences, and all. And I hope I gave you the poem all right."

He wrote "Ever yours" above his signature. But it was his leaving out the s in reminiscences that I treasure more.

Like just about everyone else I saw him in the televised proceedings of John Kennedy's inauguration. Everything went like clockwork until it was his turn. Cardinal Cushing did the invocation and Marian Anderson sang the national anthem and Vice President Johnson was sworn in between prayers by two other clergymen. Then Frost was introduced and escorted to the rostrum. It was an unusually bright day with the sunlight bouncing off the snow and he had trouble seeing the special poem he'd written for the occasion. He made a blinking attempt at four or five lines and Johnson tried to help by shielding the paper Frost was reading from with his top hat. That didn't help, so Frost put it aside and recited what he'd originally been asked to. This was "The Gift Outright" which he'd written in 1935 and was a staple in his public readings, so he could do it from memory.

John Kennedy had called him personally and asked him to make one slight change in it. Just one word, and Frost had agreed. This was in the last line of the poem.

*Such as she was, such as she would become.*

"She" was the nation and the poem was rooted in the Revolutionary War and the westward expansion which followed. Frost himself had said it was about the beginning of the end of colonialism. But the President-elect suggested that changing "would" to "will" in that last line might better suit his visionary new administration.

Frost had recited the poem too many times before. When he reached the ending he automatically said "would." Then he quickly changed it to "has" and finally blurted out "what she will become." But the applause had drowned him out by then. *The Washington Post* the next day said he'd stolen the hearts of the inaugural crowd.

I considered sending a note to the Homer Noble Farm and composed it in my mind. "If any President ever asks me to change one word of a poem I wrote a long time ago, and thus its meaning, I'll go after him with a bat." It's one of countless letters I'm glad I never got around to. But there was one about him that had to be written.

It was to *The Sunday Times of London*. I was there at the beginning of 1963 when Frost died and Robert Graves wrote their eulogy to him. Graves made it sound like they'd been lifelong friends, but according to Lawrance Thompson's biography the two only met once and that was in a bookshop in London just before Frost returned to the States. Graves referred to this encounter in his eulogy.

> "Frost, although a married man nearly forty years old, was then faced with an agonizing decision: whether or not to enlist in the British Army. He wrote a poem, 'The Road Not Taken" which ended in a sigh at having chosen the more difficult course: resisting for his family's sake the passionate temptation of battle."

My letter to the Editor of *The Sunday Times* corrected this.

> "Five years ago, Frost allowed me to film him reading this poem for use on television. He then prefaced the poem with talk of when and how he came to write it. He said it was not autobiographical, that the 'I' in the poem was his friend Edward Thomas, and that the poem was prompted by the manner in which Thomas would weigh decisions before making them. This explanation by Frost exists on film and is in the possession of the Columbia Broadcasting System in New York."

But, unfortunately, living poets always get the last word over dead ones. Graves's reply was published the following week.

"I am surprised to hear that Robert Frost denied any autobiographical sense to 'The Road Not Taken.' He made it clear enough to myself and others that it referred to his spiritual dilemma when his friend and contemporary Edward Thomas, also a married man, chose the well-trodden road to glory and the grave."

Frost probably would have thought this exchange a waste of time, that all that really matters is the poem itself, that maybe it gets an unimportant compliment from having stayed with me word-perfect so many years.

I've wanted to set all this down for a long time. I wish I'd published it while Robert Frost was still alive. I wish Mickey Cochrane was still around to see it. But way has led on to way and I've had other promises to keep.

# THE ROAD NOT TAKEN

Two roads diverged in a yellow wood,
And sorry I could not travel both
And be one traveler, long I stood
And looked down one as far as I could
To where it bent in the undergrowth

Then took the other as just as fair,
And having perhaps the better claim,
Because it was grassy and wanted wear;
Though as for that, the passing there
Had worn them really about the same,

And both that morning equally lay
In leaves no step had trodden black.
Oh, I kept the first for another day!
Yet knowing how way leads on to way
I doubted if I should ever come back.

I shall be telling this with a sigh
Somewhere ages and ages hence:
Two roads diverged in a wood, and I—
I took the one less traveled by,
And that has made all the difference.

*Mountain Interval (1916)*

# EZRA POUND
## AND
### *BREAKOUT II*

# I

Of all the incurable diseases, gambling is probably the least painful. Still, a certain amount of groaning goes with it, like having paid for the fancy Romanesque urinals in the Caesar's Palace johns. Or sometimes it's the lobby carpeting at the Dunes or Desert Inn. In my case, it's a lot of the slinky gowns that the croupiers wear in the better London casinos.

The Prince and I were regularly in attendance at one of them, and after playing at the same tables for a year or so we'd reached the state of nodding to each other. One doesn't start up a conversation with a Prince. This one especially didn't with an Arab one in 1974 when the oil crisis peaked and he was hearing threatening noises from my country.

If you subscribe to the movie channel on cable, you're bound to see a rerun of "Breakout" some night. And, if you don't blink, you'll spot my name on the screenplay credit. It's only there because the Arab Prince, who shall remain nameless, spoke to me first.

"I am a great admirer of your Alexander Hamilton," he said.

I only knew one Alexander and his last name was Pappadopolis.

"Are we talking about the face on the ten dollar bill?" I said.

"Your first Secretary of the Treasury," he said.

"And if he hadn't been killed in a duel, he might have made President, even if he was illegitimate." All this to show I knew as much about American history as he did.

"There is a new book about him," said the Prince. "It has been favorably commented upon in your Time magazine, but my aide has been unable to obtain it here."

"It happens," I said. "What's the title?"

"*The Young Hamilton*. Since I'm told that you also write books . . . " Long pause. As with all royalty, asking a favor was a venture into strange territory. ". . . I wonder if you might obtain a copy for me from the United States."

"I'll see what I can do."

"Naturally, you will be duly reimbursed."

"My treat," I said.

That night I called my agent in New York. She knew about the book. The author had won a Pulitzer, the publisher was interested in my next, if I ever finished it, and getting me a copy was no problem. I didn't leave it at that. Could the hungry publisher get the Pulitzer prizewinner to inscribe it to the Prince? Getting the spelling of his name right added another pound to my phone bill.

**The Young Hamilton** arrived with "best wishes to Prince _____ from Thomas Flexner." The Arabs had all gone home for Ramadan by then, so I had the casino manager courier it on. A few weeks later I got the invitation to collect my due reimbursement. The Prince owned about sixty horses and a four year old named Jellaby was to deliver my reward.

The Prince's aide called me on a Friday morning. If I were available to go to Newbury Racecourse the next day, a Rolls would pick me up at an appointed hour. Jellaby was running in the third race and there was a not so subtle suggestion that I show up with plenty of cash. I drew out what was left in my bank account and hit everybody I could. When the powder blue Rolls Royce arrived the following noon, I had a little over two thousand pounds in my pocket.

Newbury Racecourse is about an hour's drive from London. I was the only passenger and the chauffeur didn't speak much English. No reassurances from him. The Prince was already in his private box with the trainer of all his horses when I arrived. The trainer, Captain Ryan Price, and Brian Taylor, the jockey who was to ride Jellaby, complete my cast. Ryan Price was Irish, with a soft brogue I had to lean close to hear. As a young officer, he'd led a British commando unit in the disastrous raid on Dieppe and been decorated with the Victoria Cross or something close to it. He had a reputation for never having been sober since and for being the shrewdest trainer in the business. I immediately sought some kind of collateral from him for my two grand.

"You think Jellaby's gonna' piss the race?"

Price looked around to make sure that none but the Prince and I could hear.

"Taylor will think he's driving a Ferrari," he said. Another cautious glance over his shoulder. "Take the first show."

An explanation to those unfamiliar with British racing. At American tracks, the odds on every horse in a race change as the betting goes on and anybody who picks the winner gets whatever odds it winds up with. Across the pond, where the bookmaking racket has been legalized, one can take the odds prevailing when he makes his bet. The first show on Jellaby turned out to be six-to-one. When the race started, the odds were three-to-one. I'd taken the six with my whole wad, which was peanuts compared to what Ryan Price had riding.

It was a mile race. At the halfway point, Brian Taylor took Jellaby into the lead. It gradually lengthened. With a furlong to go, the horse was five lengths clear. I was visualizing the bookies counting out my winnings, something you should never do in advance, when Jellaby stumbled. He didn't go down, but he lurched enough to unseat his jockey.

Taylor's head hit the rail when he fell and the plastic lining of his cap didn't help. He was out cold. Jellaby crossed the finish line ten lengths ahead. For the uninformed, that doesn't count when there's no one in the saddle.

If there were any cheers for whatever won, I didn't hear them. The stands were hushed. Taylor was a popular jockey and he hadn't moved. In the silence before he did, Ryan Price's soft brogue was loud and clear. His is still the best loser's lament I've ever heard.

"If a thousand bottoms fell out of the fuckin' sky," he said, "I'd catch me wife's."

I was still pole-axed when the call came from Los Angeles that night. A few hours after the third race at Newbury, Charles Bronson threw the fifth rewrite of "Breakout" at the producers. Bronson had script approval and, because of his other commitments, shooting had to begin in ten days' time or never. There was one last chance for a writer to pull it out of the fire. And even if I didn't I'd be paid enough to make up for Jellaby's fancy footwork.

I was on the next morning's flight to L. A. The five drafts had been entrusted to a stewardess coming the other way and were waiting for me at Heathrow. I rewrote the first two scenes of the best one before we landed. Bronson approved them, plus a couple more, and agreed to make the picture provided I stayed with it and kept rewriting as we went along.

So it was that I happened to be at a housing development for senior citizens in the California desert. Development, in this case, couldn't even be called a euphemism. What our location scout had come up with looked like a circle of disabled mobile homes waiting for the next Comanche raid. But some of the exteriors had been prettied up and there were a few reluctant patches of garden. The house beautiful trophy went to the one we were using for a scene. You'll see it in the film. It's where a tough sheriff warns Bronson not to mess around with his wife. He says, "You do, and I'll tear off your head and shit in it." I want the whole world to know that this line was in a previous draft and the producers wouldn't let me change a word of it. While I sat trying to salvage other dialogue, the whole local population gathered to watch the scene being set up. Then one of them wandered over to me.

"Any chance of my getting a line?"

Even the crown of his hairless head was wrinkled and his eye pouches looked like dried figs.

"How about 'let's head them off at the pass'?" I said.

"Needs a little work."

"Sorry. The scene only has the two characters."

"I could walk past and ask one of them for a light." He added a little wheezing laugh so I wouldn't take it seriously. "I only tried," he said, "'cause I used to be in the business."

Maybe a noonday desert sun dredges up buried memories. It had been at least thirty-five years and they'd taken their toll. But I recognized him.

"You're Al Stiles."

He didn't admit it immediately, trying to place me.

"I owe you money, or what?"

"The Palace Burlesque in Buffalo was my second home," I said.

"With the longest-winded candy butchers on the circuit." He went into a sample spiel. "It may look like just a Hershey bar to you. But inside each and every one is a picture of a beautiful young model which could only be taken in gay Paree and which has been smuggled here at great expense to the management."

"Just like old times," I said.

"Imagine you remembering me."

"The best toilet seat act I ever saw," I said. No compliment could have pleased him more and he wanted one of the women in the crowd to be in on it.

"Hey Maudie! Come meet my gag writer."

I'd noticed her before. She stood out because of her skin. The cracked leather hides of the others made hers all the whiter, almost as white as her hair. When she reached us, I rewrote her complexion to English rose.

"It took your movie to drag her out of the house," said Al Stiles.

"I'm afraid I burn easily." She had retained enough of her native accent to confirm her complexion.

"I just came over from London," I said.

"Oh." A hint of nostalgia. "I imagine it's changed a bit since my day.

"He remembers my act from the Palace," said Al. "You know. The Palace in Buffalo."

"They were all the same," she said.
"What d'ya mean, the same?" You sayin' the Palace was the same as Minsky's?"

He asked it with both palms up. Everything Al Stiles said had its appropriate gesture. He wanted her to admit he was right, but I suspected that she rarely did. Instead, she turned to watch Charles Bronson coming out of his special air-conditioned trailer. As if to prove he'd worked with bigger stars. Al didn't even give him a glance.

"I still got the toilet seat," he said.

## II

When I played hookey from high school and lied about my age to the doorman at the Palace, I always pretended it was mostly to see the comedians. But I never found them any funnier than most of the audience did. Their standard routines, the courtroom slapstick and "meet me 'round the corner in half an hour" and even Fluegel Street were seemingly endless intervals between the strip-teasers. The comics got few laughs and little applause. Al Stiles, with his toilet seat, was the exception.

The seat was strapped to his head and he used the lid to make it a castanet. As the four piece pit band played a tango or mambo, he'd clatter away, his mournful face screwed up in a musical devotion last seen at Carnegie Hall. This was what made the act work, this and his total unawareness of the dancer peeling behind him. At the end of every eight bars she'd take something off and duck into the wings and the audience would yell for more. Al Stiles, of course, would take deep bows as if the ovation was for him. When the dancer got down to a G-string she never came back on and Al's last reprise was met with silence. He'd look bewildered, then hurt. He'd clap the lid against the seat twice more in defiance. Blackout!

My remembering the act was more of my doing than his. I've always been fascinated by odd-ball vaudeville turns, from blind-folded knife throwers to fire eaters. I once saw a midget upside-down, balancing himself with one forefinger on a huge beach ball. I've sometimes wondered if I might have written a masterpiece, given his dedication and willingness to fall on my face. Al Stiles's act wasn't quite in this category. But it was shameless and original. Somewhere, sometime, he'd hit on the idea and went out and bought a toilet seat and found a shoemaker to attach the leather headstraps. Not exactly a stroke of genius, maybe, but it even got applause from the shiny-pated regulars in the front row. And it made me remember him. More surprising is that since most of my attention had been on the lavender-lit stripper behind him I didn't remember Maudie.

After six takes from various angles in which Bronson was threatened with having his head removed and used as a commode, the shooting session broke up. The crew and cast packed up and headed for the motel we were all staying at and Al and Maudie had disappeared with the rest of the onlookers by then.

The next day's filming was at a deserted airstrip about ten miles away. Bronson was playing a maverick pilot who would fly anybody anywhere for a price. He only had five lines that day, but the producers wanted me there anyway. So I concentrated on scenes to come and was typing away under a huge umbrella when the cameraman started screaming that somebody was in his frame. Whoever was bicycling across the sands ignored the assistant director's loud hailer and all the waving arms didn't alter his course. Bronson said to let him know when we were ready and went back to his air conditioned trailer. Five minutes later, a gasping Al Stiles arrived and asked for me.

"I thought maybe you could use an extra stunt pilot," he said.

The sweat was rolling off his face and his T-shirt was so soaked, the red letters of Cornell on the front were beginning to run at the edges.

"You nuts?" I took the bike and he flopped down under the umbrella, still gasping. "You could get a stroke in this heat."

"Used to get them four times a day." He managed a weak smile.

"Why the hell did you do it?"
"Maudie's making her specialty tonight," he said. "I thought maybe you'd drive me back and stay for supper.

"What's her specialty?" I had to ask because I'm allergic to shellfish.

"To her it's a Lancashire Hot Pot. To me, it's just another *tsimus*."

# III

Maudie had made the parlor of their bungalow into a miniature version of Greer Garson's in *Mrs. Miniver*, a mock fireplace, warming pans on the walls, chintz chair and sofa covers, everything neat and cozy. While she bustled in and out of the small kitchen, setting up the corner table, Al produced his scrapbook.

More memories. The photographs of the headliners didn't have to be smuggled in from Paris. The poses were coquettish, but the feather boas were expertly placed. All were autographed to Al, but I didn't need the signatures to recognize them. Ann Corio, Rose La Rose, Charmalne, Gladys Fox, Georgia Southern. I wanted to bask in their beauty, but Al turned to the pages with the comedians. He'd played with the biggest. He'd stooged for Rags Ragland and Willie Howard and been on the receiving end of shellacked pigs' bladders wielded by Red Skelton. Skelton had made the jump to the silver screen, but Al forgave him that. Otherwise, and I quote him exactly, "Any of 'em had more talent in their left nut than all your Oscar winners put together."

Then he turned to the most prized photograph of all. It was of him doing his specialty with the semi-nude dancer a background statue. If he hadn't told me, I still wouldn't have known it was Maudie. She happened to be bringing us a plate of celery and olives when he did.

"I never stripped before I married him," she said.

He waited until she went back to the kitchen.

"Just between us," he said, "it always bothered me."

"Couldn't you have hired someone to do it?"

"Maybe you also remember something called the Depression."

Another page, another photograph.

"Recognize her in this one?"

The picture was postcard sized, its original sepia tint faded. The little girl was costumed as a street waif and knelt at the feet of a Victorian dandy as if begging him for a farthing. It was studio posed with the photographers names, Oakley and Sidebottom, engraved beneath.

"They don't make them like that any more," said Al.

"And this goes with it."

The programme, cellophane covered on the album page, was from the Theatre Royal, Glossop. The cast list was surrounded by local advertisements. Geo. W. Casey, High Class

Baker and Confectioner, gave "Special Attention to Family Orders." Thomas Shoebridge, Progressive Hatter and Gentleman's Outfitter, received customers at 2 Norfolk Street. Julien Mitchell, Dentist, was at number 12 and Waterhouse, Chemist, at number 32. The play was THE RICH AND POOR OF LONDON, "A Realistic Drama of the Present Day" and the character of Seadrift was performed by Miss Maude Midgely.

"How about that?" said Al, pointing to her name.

"Now I'm really impressed."

"You ain't seen nuthin' yet." The variation on Al Jolson's famous line led to the next photo. Maudie, in top hat and tails, couldn't have been more than fifteen.

"Male impersonators were big then," he said. "Now it's the other way around. That's what they call progress."

"Dinner is served," said Maudie.

A stew by any other name. Lancashire Hot Pot turned out to be chunks of mutton mingled with carrots and turnips and the whole lidded with sliced potatoes. It look innocent enough before I tasted it.

"I add quite a bit of cayenne pepper," said Maudie, during my coughing fit.

"Also known as gunpowder," said Al. He tapped the top of his head. "How d'ya think I lost my hair?"

"Hardly." Her English accent was getting more pronounced. "That ridiculous skull harness rubbed it off."

It was more good-natured than it sounds and the fire in my head from the pepper was burning low. I was glad I'd accepted their invitation.

"Do you know any other writers?" Maudie became the perfect hostess showing an interest in her guest.

"A few." I name-dropped a couple. "Norman Mailer . . . Gore Vidal."

"Never heard of 'em," said Al. "How about Mickey Spillane?"

"Or Ezra Pound," said Maudie.

The jump threw me and Al didn't give me time to recover.

"Now don't start on that son-of-a-bitch."

"I merely asked if he knew him."

"Who'd want to know that lousy Jew-hating bastard?"

"I never met him," I said.

I hoped that would end it, but the rose in Maudie's cheeks had turned from pink to deep red and she wasn't letting go.

"Do you happen to know if Mr. Pound is still alive?"

"Mister Pound? You still call that traitor, Mister?"

"I think he died last year," I said.

"A hundred years too late," said Al.

"I didn't know he was dead." Her sadness was genuine.

"I used to have a book of his poems." She looked at her husband accusingly. "But someone threw it away."

"Never!" Al's raised right hand was straight out of the courtroom slapstick act. "She forgot to pack the goddam thing."

"Where?"

"How do I know where? Someplace between Duluth and Des Moines." Al's dentures were fighting a piece of mutton.

"I used to read them," she said. "I didn't understand them, but I liked reading them."

"He was a no good, anti-Semitic cocksucker," said Al.

"I still remember some of the lines." Al got another accusing look. "Those weren't left behind."

"So help me," This time Al's hand was on his heart."

"'I have sung women in three cities'," she recited.

"Sure. Peoria, Poughkeepsie and Podunk."

"He was a gentleman," said Maudie.

It was up to me to play peacemaker. Asking people about themselves is usually the best way, but this time took some extra prodding. Al gave in first, his life story fitting into a familiar nutshell. In Hell's Kitchen, a Jewish boy grew up to be a prize-fighter, a gangster or a comedian.

"And I always hated the sight of blood." Al topped his own line. "So I became a musician."

"Some instrument," said Maudie.

Al lifted his napkin, did a double-take at his fly and breathed a sigh of relief.

"She had me scared for a minute."

Ezra Pound was gone and their customary banter returned.

"Next stop, Glossop," said Al.

It was a town near Manchester where Maudie'd been born and which her mother had been determined to get them both out of. Her father had been a minor government clerk and like so many men of that ilk enjoyed hitting his wife. Maudie had come in for her share of lumps and, though he'd been dead fifty years, she still hated him. THE RICH AND POOR OF LONDON had provided the escape. The girl playing Seadrift had come down with influenza. Maudie never found out how her mother persuaded the company manager to give her the part.

"I'll give you one guess." Al offered it to me.

When the troupe left Glossop, Maudie and her mother left with it and never looked back. Her mother's small sayings later took them to London. Her mother worked as a seamstress and she'd taken singing and dancing lessons.

"This part always chokes me up." Al started humming, *Hearts and Flowers*.

The male impersonation act was her mother's idea. But young girls in top hats and tails were no longer a novelty and bookings were scarce. Mrs. Midgely decided that their future was in New York. She had a distant cousin in Albany who offered hospitality but forgot to mention how far Albany was from Broadway. Still, it was the state capital and had plenty of theatres. Maudie worked fairly steadily, usually performing between showings of silent films.

"I used to do Dan Leno," she said. I pretended to have heard of him. "Not that it meant anything in Albany."

"Enter the travelling salesman," said Al. He'd managed not to interrupt for longer than usual. "Buttons, yet. Can you imagine a guy spending his life travelling around and selling buttons?"

"Some people like to travel," I said.

"And my mother was one of them," said Maudie.

Exit Mrs. Midgely with the salesman, and the daughter she'd left behind didn't get along with the distant cousin. Maudie was ripe for another escape and The Great Hannibal was an escapologist.

"I caught his act, once." Al held his nose. "He couldn't get out of his shoes without untying the laces."

But he'd had thirty weeks of solid bookings. The act was all him, with another young girl and Maudie as prop handlers and window dressing. All the bookings turned out to be in tank towns, from Olean, New York to Crawfordsville, Indiana. It was in Crawfordsville one January night that the other girl got The Great Hannibal to a Justice of the Peace and Maudie was left behind again. She hadn't been paid for the final week and her room rent was due.

"So little Nell was thrown out into the cold, cold night," said Al.

"And met Prince Charming," said Maudie.

That did it. He got up from the table, threw his napkin on the floor and went to sulk in his scrapbook.

"That wasn't very far from the truth," said Maudie.

She'd been sixteen and penniless and didn't know a soul in town. Or so she'd thought. Cold, cold night was putting it mildly. A blizzard had emptied the streets she aimlessly walked. Then the solitary figure of Ezra Pound appeared.

Her memory faltered at this point. He'd claimed to recognize her, but not from the stage. He'd had a room in the theatrical boarding house the first few days she stayed there. He said she'd been with some other performers who'd had a snack there after a show.

"Probably fuckin' Fascist hotpot," mumbled Al.

Pound had moved to another house which the Wabash College president thought more fitting to his position as a teacher. He'd braved the wind and snow that night to mail a letter to his father. He was convinced that fate had arranged their meeting and insisted she come back to his room to thaw out. He'd apologized for not having much to offer her to eat.

"Just his dick," said Al.

A small gas fire had warmed her while she ate the few biscuits he'd had. And there'd been a bar of chocolate, too.

"Smuggled in at great expense to the management," said Al.

"And he wouldn't hear of my not sleeping in his bed."

"I'll bet he wouldn't."

We were both ignoring Al's interpolations. Ezra Pound had completely upstaged him. I probed her for details, but they were fragmented. He'd had a massive crop of hair. She was particular about the color, closer to carrot than red, and there'd been the beginning of a goatee, and his eyes almost matched the green of his velvet jacket. She was less definite about what he'd said. He'd kept his voice down because of his landladies, but he'd ranted away about everything wrong in the world, including what had just been done to her.

"Funny," she said. "There was only one piece that's stayed with me.

"And what's that?"

"He was teaching in this Presbyterian college, you see."

She took her time to get his words exact. "It's easier to teach French and Spanish to Presbyterians than to get anyone to think clearly."

"He's known to have made a lot of statements for shock value," I said.

"But he was different." Maudie said it quietly so Al couldn't hear. "Any other man that night . . ." I may have imagined a touch of wistfulness in her hesitation. "But he spent the whole night on the floor in his overcoat. I swear he did."

"What's goin' on over there?" Al could no longer stand being left out.

"'I have sung women in three cities'." She recited it across the room to him. "'But it is all one. I will sing of the sun.'"

"What the hell she talkin' about?" Al appealed to me.

"You can't throw away the lines I know by heart," she said. Then she turned to me. "Do you know what they mean?"

"Sorry. It would just be a guess."

She'd been awakened by shrieking spinster sisters. The landladies had come to tidy the room after seeing their only boarder leave to teach his first morning class. One kept screaming insults at her while she quickly dressed. The other hurried to inform the president of Wabash College.

"It wasn't until I got outside," said Maudie, "that I found the twenty dollars Mr. Pound had put in my pocketbook."

"That was a lot in those days," said Al, "even for all night."

"He must have lost his teaching job because of me." Maudie's remorse was obviously long felt. "I know what he did during the war and what happened to him afterwards." All coloring had drained from her face and she touched a cheek with trembling fingers as if to restore it. "But maybe if he hadn't lost his teaching job . . ."

## IV

The small talk over the coffee and chocolate ice cream was strained. We'd joined Al across the room, but he was still brooding and shrugged off our attempts to bring him out of it. Then Maudie hit on the right one.

"I'm sure our guest would like to see your act once more.

"No truer word," I said.

It took just a little more coaxing to make him get the toilet seat out of the closet.

"Where do we get a beautiful broad to peel behind me?"

"We'll dispense with that part,' she said.

"I'll imagine Rose La Rose," I said.

"Maudie had better tits."

He strapped the toilet seat to his head and she put a record on the turntable before sitting next to me on the chintz-covered sofa. They'd obviously done this many times before. It was a Xavier Cugat number and Al's clapping of the toilet seat lid was in perfect synch' with Cugat's Ay-ya, Ay-ya. But he'd added a new finish since those Palace days. No two final claps of defiance at the audience. The song climaxed in a torrent of notes and he matched them all the way, whipping off his headgear and taking his bow a split second after the last one.

"Still the best toilet seat player in the world," I said. I said it over Maudie's and my applause, keeping it flippant and pretending not to notice the tears in her eyes. Nothing could follow his performance, but I waited another ten minutes before using the excuse of having a tough scene to rewrite before morning.

They stood in the doorway watching me drive away. A full moon and the distant buttes provided a perfect backdrop for my final sight of them, of an old man who'd tried so hard to make people laugh and an old woman who'd so influenced the life of Ezra Pound, standing together so frail and small, winding up life's act on such an unsuitable stage.

At that time, like Maudie Stiles, I didn't understand most of the poetry of Pound's that I'd read. Since then, I've read and understood much more. I've also learned more about him. Those who knew him well helped. Yeats felt Pound had chosen the wrong mask with which to face the broken mirrors and anonymous beings of the world and Wyndham Lewis undoubtedly captured part of him in his story, "Doppelganger." But Maudie Stiles had helped, too.

My favorite lines of Pound's are from an early poem and I'd like to believe they were amongst those she'd memorized. It may be asking too much, but Jellaby taught me never to underestimate the unlikely. So I'll continue to hope that Maudie remembered.

> *In the slow float of different light and deep,*
> *No! there is nothing! In the whole and all,*
> *Nothing that's quite your own.*
> *Yet this is you.*

Just for the record, Ezra Pound was dismissed from the faculty of Wabash College in January, 1908, and left for Europe the following month.

(From a letter by Ezra Pound to William Carlos Williams.)

London
21, October, 1908

Again as to the unconstrained vagabondism. If anybody ever shuts you in Indiana for four months and you don't at least write some unconstrained something or other, I'd give up hope for your salvation. Again, if you ever get degraded, branded with infamy, etc. for feeding a person who needs food, (1) you will probably rise up and bless the present and sacred name of Madame Grundy for all her holy hypocrisy. I am not getting bitter. I have been more than blessed for my kindness and the few shekels cast on the water have come back ten fold and I have no fight with anybody.

## About The Author

Elliott Baker was born in 1922 in Buffalo, New York, graduated from Indiana University, and was an infantry rifleman in World War II. His works have been published in numerous countries and languages. These include his novels, *A Fine Madness* (1964), *The Penny Wars* (1968), *Pocock & Pitt* (1971), *Klynt's Law* (1976), *And We Were Young* (1979), *Unhealthful Air* (1988), and *Doctor Lopez* (1995). A partial autobiography, *Unrequited Loves*, was published in 1974 and a collection of essays, *Bardolatry*, in 1992. He has written for both television and motion pictures (receiving an Emmy nomination for his teleplay *The Entertainer*), and his fiction and non-fiction have appeared in publications ranging from *GQ Magazine* to *The Elizabethan Review*. In 1997, Indiana University awarded him its highest honor given to an alumnus, The President's Medal for Excellence "for making a positive and profound impact in the literary field."